REVENUE SHARING AND THE CITY

REVENUE SHARING AND THE CITY

Walter W. Heller, Richard Ruggles
Lyle C. Fitch, Carl S. Shoup, Harvey E. Brazer

Edited by Harvey S. Perloff and Richard P. Nathan

*Based on a conference sponsored by
the Committee on Urban Economics
of Resources for the Future, Inc.*

Published for Resources for the Future, Inc.
by The Johns Hopkins Press

71820

RESOURCES FOR THE FUTURE, INC.

1755 Massachusetts Avenue, N.W., Washington, D.C. 20036

Resources for the Future is a non-profit corporation for research and
education in the development, conservation, and use of natural
resources. It was established in 1952 with the co-operation of the Ford
Foundation and its activities since then have been financed by grants
from that Foundation. Part of the work of Resources for the Future
is carried out by its resident staff, part supported by grants to
universities and other non-profit organizations. Unless otherwise
stated, interpretations and conclusions in RFF publications are those
of the authors; the organization takes responsibility for the selection
of significant subjects for study, the competence of the researchers,
and their freedom of inquiry.

This book is one of RFF's regional and urban studies, which are
directed by Harvey S. Perloff. The conference on which the book is
based was held in Washington, D.C., January 26–28, 1967.

RFF editors: Henry Jarrett, Vera W. Dodds, Nora E. Roots,
Sheila M. Ekers

CONTENTS

	Page
Preface	vii

I. THE PAPERS

A Sympathetic Reappraisal of Revenue Sharing
Walter W. Heller — 3

The Federal Government and Federalism
Richard Ruggles — 39

II. THE DISCUSSION

Reflections on the Case for the Heller Plan
Lyle C. Fitch — 75

Federal Grants to Cities, Direct and Indirect
Carl S. Shoup — 92

Comments on Block Grants to the States
Harvey E. Brazer — 100

Rebuttal Comments
Walter W. Heller
Richard Ruggles — 107

v

PREFACE

This volume is the product of a conference session that "took off" and developed a life of its own.

Revenue sharing was one of thirteen topics covered by a conference on *Issues in Urban Economics*, sponsored by the Committee on Urban Economics of Resources for the Future, Inc.* In selecting a single policy issue for concentrated attention among

---

* The Committee on Urban Economics, established in 1959 to advance the field of urban economics through fellowships, research grants and conferences, has been supported by grants from the Ford Foundation. Its membership includes economists and other social scientists from universities and research organizations who have been involved in the analysis of urban problems for many years: Harold J. Barnett, Washington University; Donald J. Bogue, University of Chicago; Alan K. Campbell, Syracuse University; F. Stuart Chapin, Jr., University of North Carolina; Joseph L. Fisher, Resources for the Future, Inc.; Lyle C. Fitch, Institute of Public Administration; William L. Garrison, University of Illinois at Chicago Circle; Walter W. Heller, University of Minnesota; Werner Z. Hirsch, University of California, Los Angeles; Edgar M. Hoover, University of Pittsburgh; Eric E. Lampard, University of Wisconsin; Julius Margolis, Stanford University; Selma J. Mushkin, George Washington University–Council of State Governments; Richard Ruggles, Yale University; Howard G. Schaller, Indiana University; Wilbur R. Thompson, Wayne State University; Arthur M. Weimer, Indiana University; Lowdon Wingo, Jr., Resources for the Future, Inc.; Harvey S. Perloff, Resources for the Future, Inc. (Chairman).

the many of potential interest to urbanists (most of the conference being devoted to more academic subjects), the revenue-sharing theme was chosen because it touches on so many basic questions in our urban future: (1) the future demand for urban public services; (2) the costs of supplying such services at varying levels of excellence; (3) the capacity of urban communities to raise needed revenues; (4) the appropriate division of functions among the various levels of government; (5) the capacity of the states to be helpful to their urban communities and the future of state governments in general; (6) the relative advantages and disadvantages of federal block grants as compared with categorical grants, and a host of other intriguing issues. The fact that one of the members of the Committee on Urban Economics, Walter Heller, had been one of the originators of the best known proposal for revenue sharing added to the attractiveness of the theme.

At the time the conference was planned, revenue sharing[1] seemed to be a good "academic" subject. The Heller-Pechman proposal had received some attention for a brief period of time, but interest had flagged and the issue seemed safely relegated to a "for-future-reference" category. This appeared to be a good subject to demonstrate to fledgling urban economists how established economists go about analyzing a policy issue; the approach would be more instructive than the content itself. Heller was in-

---

[1] Revenue sharing refers to various proposals to have the federal government provide a new form of general and less conditional financial aid to state and local governments.

vited to present a paper outlining the case for revenue sharing; Richard Ruggles, of Yale University, undertook to present an opposing view; two experts on finance and urban development, Lyle Fitch and Carl Shoup, agreed to comment on the two papers.

Conference planning, like other kinds of planning, is subject to the unexpected. When the conference convened late in January 1967, revenue sharing had become a subject of intense political interest and heated discussion. A number of bills on revenue sharing had been introduced in Congress; governors and mayors were taking open positions on the Heller-Pechman proposal; Sunday supplements were discussing the subject with erudition. Even though the conference was limited to a small group of scholars, the Committee found itself overwhelmed with requests for the papers on revenue sharing. Further, it turned out that the two official discussants, chosen for their expertise rather than their stand on the subject, took positions essentially opposing revenue sharing without strings attached. To balance matters somewhat, Harvey Brazer was invited to present his views on the subject, and on an extremely important feature of the revenue-sharing plan, the "pass-through" to localities, Brazer espoused still a third position. Revenue sharing thus passed far beyond the format of the conference as a whole and took on a life of its own.

Because interest in revenue sharing was immediate and extended beyond a scholarly concern with urban economics, it was thought useful to publish the papers on the revenue-sharing theme separately from the rest of the conference papers. In this way, they could be made available to a broad readership well in advance of the conference proceedings. The papers were revised, in some cases substantially, for publication in this book.

Richard P. Nathan, of The Brookings Institution, who has written perceptively on the revenue-sharing theme, agreed to help with the editing chore. Among other contributions, he suggested some materials on urban problems for inclusion in the Heller paper.

Harvey S. Perloff

I

THE PAPERS

A SYMPATHETIC REAPPRAISAL OF REVENUE SHARING

*Walter W. Heller**

Looking beyond current rising Vietnam costs, big deficits, and contingent tax increases, one can visualize an $8 billion annual automatic growth in federal revenues generating new leeway for fiscal dividends—tax cuts, tax sharing, program increases —if Vietnam demands level off. If rising revenues are not to hold the economy back under such circumstances, we need to get our bets down promptly on the competing entrants in the fiscal drag race.

If contingency fiscal planning is to be meaningful, it has to move from academic discussion to the hard process of defining the alternatives more sharply and setting the dollar or percentage priorities that flow not just from our assumptions about projected conditions of the U.S. economy but from our ordering of policy objectives and values.

---

* Professor of Economics, University of Minnesota; former Chairman, Council of Economic Advisers.

I wish to acknowledge Richard P. Nathan's valued assistance in the preparation of this paper, especially the section dealing with the pass-through to local government. Also, since my "reappraisal" here is not really at odds with my appraisal in Chapter 3 of *New Dimensions of Political Economy* (Harvard University Press) published in 1966, the reader will not be surprised to learn that this paper owes a considerable debt to that chapter.

Consideration of the size and form of the state-local stake in this process goes forward in a setting of a growing national debate over revenue sharing. In the course of this debate, some of the issues have been blurred or confused by the welter of competing plans, variants, and even mutants now marching together under the tax-sharing banner. So a brief statement of what the tax-sharing plan is—and what it is not— seems desirable at the outset.[1] Then, to bring some of the central issues back into clearer focus, I will review the tax-sharing or general-assistance approach in terms of the ends we are trying to serve in our search for a better fiscal balance in our federalism. And, finally, I want to re-examine the claims of local government, especially the urban centers, to an earmarked slice of the shared revenues.

In suggesting that some issues have been blurred in the debate of the past three years, I don't want to be misunderstood. The debate itself is good, indeed essential. It has brought to the front pages and to both ends of Pennsylvania Avenue a degree of concern for the vitality and financial health of state-local government and for the federal government's responsibilities on this score that has not been matched in many a decade. This reawakened and self-conscious concern over the problems and values of federalism is already reflected in several pieces of legislation, in closer White House liaison with governors and

---

[1] An extremely helpful reference document on the various different proposed tax-sharing plans is Maureen McBreen, "Federal Tax Sharing: Historical Development and Arguments for and against Recent Proposals" (Library of Congress Legislative Reference Service, January 30, 1967).

mayors, and in explicit recognition of state-local claims to a share of the extra federal fiscal dividend after Vietnam.[2] To the extent that the revenue-sharing proposal has contributed to these developments, it has already served an important part of its purpose.

The Criteria and the Plan

Even in a quick review of the tax-sharing plan, we need to remind ourselves of the tests and criteria that new instruments for channeling federal funds to the states should be designed to meet. Ideally, any new plan or approach should supply funds in ways that will

—not only relieve immediate pressures on state-local treasuries, but make their revenues more responsive to economic growth;

—build up the vitality, efficiency, and fiscal independence of state-local governments;

—increase the progressivity of our federal-state-local tax system;

—reduce economic inequalities and fiscal disparities among the states;

---

[2] The President, in his 1967 Economic Report, instructed the heads of relevant agencies, under the leadership of the Council of Economic Advisers, "to begin at once a major and coordinated effort to review our readiness (to adjust to peace)." He requested that these officials consider, among other possibilities, "the future direction of Federal financial support to our State and local governments." In the latter connection, a subcommittee—one of nine—has been set up and is now working to examine possibilities in this field. *Economic Report of the President*, January 1967, pp. 23–24.

—stimulate state and local tax efforts;

—ensure that the plight of local, and especially urban, governments will be given full weight.

The device that can serve all of these ends simultaneously has yet to be developed. But I believe that per capita revenue sharing, or some allied form of unfettered general assistance, will come closer to doing so than any alternative proposed thus far.

The core of the revenue-sharing plan is the regular distribution of a specified portion of the federal individual income tax to the state primarily on the basis of population and with next to no strings attached or, at least, no hamstrings attached. This distribution would be over and above existing and future conditional grants.

A percentage set-aside. The federal government would each year set aside and distribute to the states an eventual 2 per cent of the federal individual income tax base (the amount reported as net taxable income by all individuals). This would mean that, under its existing rate schedule, the federal government would collect 2 percentage points in each bracket for the states and 12 to 68 percentage points for itself. In 1967, for example, 2 points would have yielded the states about $6 billion, or 10 per cent, of total federal personal income tax collections.

Use of a trust fund. The sums so collected for the states would be placed in a trust fund from which periodic distributions would be made. The trust fund would be the natural vehicle for handling such earmarked funds, just as it is in the case of payroll taxes for social security purposes and motor vehicle and gasoline taxes for the highway program. It would also underscore the fact that the states receive the funds as a matter of right, free from the uncertainties and hazards of the annual appropriation process.

Per capita distribution. The states would share the income tax proceeds on the basis of population. Per capita sharing would transfer some funds from states with high incomes—and therefore high per capita income tax liabilities—to low-income, low-tax states. If the modest equalization implicit in per capita sharing is deemed too limited, 10 to 15 per cent of the shared revenue can be set aside for supplements to states with low per capita income or with a high incidence of poverty, dependency, or urbanization.

Pass-through. Whether to leave the fiscal claims of the localities to the mercies of the political process and the institutional realities of each state or to require a pass-through to them is not an easy question. Previously, I had left this question open, but I now conclude that the legitimate—and pressing—claims of local government require explicit recognition in the basic formula of revenue sharing.

No hamstrings attached. States would be given wide latitude—nearly complete freedom—in the use of their revenue shares. Yet, the Congress would not simply be providing "stump money," i.e., putting money on the stump and running the other way. Without sullying the basic no-strings character of these grants, one would

—ask the states to meet the usual public auditing, accounting, and reporting requirements on public funds;

—perhaps even broadly restrict the use of the funds to education, health, welfare, and community development programs—or at least provide that they not be spent for highways (which are already financed through a special trust fund).

An effort index. Unlike the federal crediting device, a straight tax-sharing device contains no automatic spur to greater state-local tax effort. But such a spur could be built in by weighting the per capita grants to each state by the ratio of that state's tax effort to the average tax effort in the country—tax effort being defined as the ratio of state-local general revenues to personal income. An interesting and rather mixed bag of above-and-below-par states emerges by this standard. For example, in 1964:

- Louisiana, New Mexico, and North Dakota would have had effort indexes of 120 or above.
- Nine states would have had an index of 85 or less: Connecticut, Delaware, Illinois, Maryland, Missouri, New Jersey, Ohio, Pennsylvania, and Virginia.

Revenue impact. The federal individual income tax base will reach the $300 billion mark in 1967. So each per cent of the base would provide the states with $3 billion a year. If 2 per cent of the federal income tax base were being distributed in 1967, the grant would be $6 billion, or roughly $30 per capita. Without taking account of special equalization features, this would mean, for example, grants of about $60 million for Arkansas, $560 million for California,

8

$60 million for Colorado, $320 million for Illinois, $180 million for Massachusetts, $110 million each for Louisiana and Minnesota, $120 million for Missouri, $20 million for Montana, $560 million for New York, $150 million for North Carolina, $360 million for Pennsylvania, $30 million for Utah, $130 million for Virginia, and $120 million for Wisconsin.

In spite of four recessions, the grants under the proposed plan would have risen in every year since 1950 except for a miniscule decline of one-tenth of 1 per cent in 1958. The income tax base, to which the allotments are keyed, has grown from $65 billion in 1946 to $128 billion in 1955, to $210 billion in 1963, and the estimated $300 billion in 1967—and has risen from 31 per cent of gross national product in 1946 to an estimated 38 per cent in 1967. By 1972, the federal income tax base should grow to $425 billion (assuming a 6-per-cent annual growth in money gross national product, and the income tax base growing 20 per cent faster than gross national product). So a 2-per-cent-of-base share would reach $8½ billion by 1972. Truly, a share in the federal income tax would be a share in U.S. economic growth.

The competing claims of federal tax cuts and expenditure increases would probably require that the plan start modestly (perhaps at one-half of 1 per cent or 1 per cent) and build up gradually to 2 per cent over three or four years. This gradual build-up would enable the states to program their own fiscal affairs more efficiently.

The federal commitment to share income tax revenues with the states would be a contractual one in the sense of being payable—at whatever percentage Congress provided—through thick and thin, through surplus and deficit in the federal budget. The plan could hardly have its claimed advantages of stiffening and strengthening state and local governments if they were last in the fiscal line, ever fearful that federal deficits would deprive them of their "cut" of the federal income tax.

The very nature of the proposal calls for them to be first in line for their designated share of the income tax, even if it means that the federal government has to bear the brunt of periodic deficit financing—which, indeed, it can do much more readily and appropriately than state and local governments.

Unrelenting Fiscal Pressures

In spite of dramatic postwar growth in categorical aids as well as state-local tax revenues, there has been no let-up in the intense fiscal pressures on states and localities. Some recent projections seem to suggest that prosperity in state-local finance is just around the corner, that spending pressures will relent while revenues grow.[3]

---

[3] By no means all projections are so optimistic. Pechman foresees a $15 billion gap between projected expenditures and receipts by 1970 (Joseph A. Pechman, "Financing State and Local Government," in American Bankers Association, *Proceedings of a Symposium on Federal Taxation*, 1965; also published as Reprint No. 103, Brookings Institution, 1965). Dick Netzer has projected a $10 billion gap, on somewhat different assumptions, for 1970 (in an unpublished manuscript for the Committee for Economic Development, "State-Local Finance in the Next Decade," August 1965).

Yet Mushkin and Lupo see no gap under their "high-revenue

Unmet needs. But before anyone reaches the complacent conclusion that state and local governments can meet future needs without undue restraint, let him knock on any fiscal door or scratch any fiscal surface at the state and local levels. Let him probe the reality that lies behind and beyond the statistics he uses as his point of departure. And let him look beyond today's scope and quality of services to the aspirations that grow out of abundance. Let him find a single major city or state that can meet these aspirations without fiscal heroics.

For that matter, let him look around his own community. In his own suburb he will find unmet needs for school facilities, sewers, sidewalks, street lights, green space, more frequent garbage and trash collection. Or in his central city, let him look closer at the rutted streets and crumbling curbs; at the deteriorating parks and miserable housing in the urban ghettoes; at delinquency, crime, and poverty. Are the

---

assumption," which includes $22 billion of federal aid and $15 billion of gross borrowing, and only a small gap under their "low revenue assumption." Selma J. Mushkin and Gabrielle C. Lupo, "Project '70: Projecting the State-Local Sector," The George Washington University, State-Local Finances Project. (Summarized in *Review of Economics and Statistics*, Vol. 49 [May 1967].) The CED, in *A Fiscal Program for a Balanced Federalism*, June 1967, pp. 23–27, also makes rather sanguine revenue-expenditure projections for 1975, but recognizes that the actual results will depend on "improvements in scope and quality of public services." The Tax Foundation projection is the most optimistic. It foresees a $5 billion surplus in 1975, assuming improvement in scope and quality at 1960–65 rates, a doubling of federal aid, and no aggregate increase in state-local tax rates. (See *Fiscal Outlook for State and Local Government to 1975*, Tax Foundation, 1966.)

costs of meeting these urgent needs truly reflected in the projections? And lest he be misled by some temporary surpluses growing out of the unexpected surge in revenues from an economy overheated by Vietnam, let him look dead ahead at the near-doubling of higher education expenditures in the next five years, at the crying needs for better prisons and mental hospitals, and at the fight against air, water, and land pollution, which has only just begun.

And we are all well advised to remember that underneath the aggregates and averages lie huge disparities among individual units. Do the projections allow for the tendency of rising revenues in the more affluent communities to disappear in higher standards of state-local services, while the pinch grows ever tighter on the below-average communities?

Statistical projections of needs and resources are, of course, essential for planning, for defining our problems. But projections are not goals. Our fiscal planning has to prepare for the worst—for the minimum demanded by quantitative projections—while it plans for the best—for the maximum demanded by our qualitative goals and hopes in a framework of abundance.

Statistical projections alone tend to beg the question. That question, as noted early in our discussion, is not *whether* states and localities can make ends meet, but *on what terms*. On terms that just cover the irresistible minimum or that fulfill our hopes? On terms that force our federal-state-local tax system into a more and more regressive mold or that protect its progressivity? On terms that perpetuate the great inequalities among the states or that steadily reduce them? On terms that will enable state and local governments to become vital and creative units in the machine of federalism, or just overburdened service stations?

State-local response. State and local officials can bring some vivid testimony to bear on these questions. As Pechman has put it,

> State officials would be amazed to learn that their fiscal problems are almost over. Between 1959 and 1966, every state but one raised rates or adopted a new major tax; there were 230 tax rate increases and nineteen new tax adoptions in this period. This year, the governors asked their legislatures for $3 billion in additional revenues.[4]

As if to bear out Pechman's point, the states have been busy enacting new and increased taxes. In the first six months of 1967, Michigan and Nebraska enacted personal and corporate income taxes, and West Virginia, a corporate income tax; Minnesota and Nebraska added sales taxes; a large number of states raised income, sales, gasoline, and cigarette taxes.[5] Wealthy California enacted a billion dollars in added taxes.

Even if we give states and localities an A or A-plus for their tax efforts, it does not follow that they have done all they should. Until the laggard states and localities raise their tax efforts to the levels of the leaders, until state-local tax administration is strengthened, until local government structure

---

[4] Joseph A. Pechman, reply to Melville J. Ulmer in "The People's Forum," *The Progressive*, June 1967.

[5] *New York Times*, June 27, 1967.

is reformed, one's praise must be qualified. But to infer that the federal government should withhold broader fiscal support of the states until they have taken these steps, as some critics do, not only ignores the strenuous tax efforts they are already making, but fails to see that greater federal support and growing state-local reform can go hand-in-hand—indeed, that such support can facilitate or even stimulate reform.[6]

The role of conditional grants. In distributing future fiscal dividends, the federal government can and should give high priority to categorical aids. One can assume that their dramatic growth will continue. They tripled in the 1950's, reaching $7 billion by 1960. They are well on the way to tripling again by 1970, as is reflected in the President's request of $17.4 billion in categorical aids for fiscal 1968.

In appraising the relative role of conditional and unconditional grants, one must be clear on the distinction between the defects or flaws in the application of our existing grant-in-aid system—those which can presumably be overcome by improvements in the system, and those which are intrinsic to the conditional grant-in-aid instrument.

Keen awareness of the limitations in practice was expressed in testimony before the Senate Subcommittee on Intergovernmental Relations last year by Charles L. Schultze, Director of the Bureau of the Budget. He put his finger on such problems as

---

[6] Congressman Henry S. Reuss strikes an interesting compromise. His bill (H.R. 1166) would provide for a general-assistance sharing plan, but the actual transfer of revenues to state-local governments would be made contingent on submission of satisfactory plans for reform of state-local governmental structures.

—proliferation of programs to a total of 162 by early-1966, under 399 separate authorizations;

—excessive categorization of grants which, together with direct negotiations between individual bureaus and their counterparts in state-local governments, have led to bypassing of governors and mayors and weakening of their control over their own administrations;

—the difficulties in co-ordination and broad policy planning by federal, state, and local governments that result from the fragmentation of grants and appropriations.[7]

These problems obviously call for reforms internal to the grant-in-aid system. They are also relevant to the case for shared taxes. They suggest that there may be significant limits, in terms of efficiency in practical application, to increased reliance on central direction of resources through conditional federal grants-in-aid.

But to conclude, as some authors of tax-sharing proposals and bills do, that tax shares should be substituted for grants-in-aid not only goes too far, but misses the point. Categorical grants-in-aid are indispensable instruments for federal support of state-local services infused with the national interest. Where there are large spillover effects—i.e., where inadequate education, health, anti-poverty, and anti-pollution programs in one area will mean costs

---

[7] Charles L. Schultze, Hearings before the Subcommittee on Intergovernmental Relations of the Committee on Government Operations, U.S. Senate, 89th Cong., 2nd Sess., Part I: The Federal Level, pp. 390–91.

inflicted on the rest of the country—there is a compelling economic case for earmarked grants-in-aid for specific purposes. In striking the cost-benefit balance, each community counts only its own benefits from such programs, ignoring the important benefits that accrue to other communities in a highly mobile society like ours. Unless the federal government steps in to represent the national interest in the benefits derived from these state-local services, the latter would be badly undernourished. So, grants-in-aid must continue to be our major reliance in transferring federal funds to the states.

The role of unconditional grants. Beyond support of *specific* state-local services with large spillover effects, the interests of a healthy and balanced federalism also call for federal support of the *general* state-local enterprise. Beset by large inequalities in fiscal capacity, by the debilitating effect of interstate competition and limited jurisdiction—often compounded by the suction effect of the matching requirements of categorical grants—state-local government is forced to strike the fiscal balance at levels of services well below the needs and desires of its citizens. The lack of a fiscal instrument to serve this broader purpose—to raise their general capacity to serve, especially in the poorer states, and to do so in ways that foster decentralized discretion and responsibility—is a major gap in the fiscal structure of U.S. federalism. Tax sharing could fill it.

So the fiscal case for the tax-sharing, or general-assistance, or untied-grants approach goes well beyond the purely *quantitative* consideration of limited state-local resources. It rests also on the *qualitative*

need for a separate instrument to achieve a separate
goal, for general-assistance grants designed

—to finance improvements in the quality and level
of state-local services, especially in the poorer
states;
—to stimulate the exercise of state-local initiative
and responsibility as part of the national interest
in revitalizing state and local government.

Revitalizing State-Local Government

In a basic sense, the case for shared taxes begins
with the conviction that strong and financially viable
states (interpreted to mean "state-local governments") are essential to (a) a healthy federalism and
(b) optimality in the performance of public services.

In part, this simply expresses the traditional faith
in pluralism and decentralization, diversity, innovation, and experimentation. For those who lack that
faith—for died-in-the-wool Hamiltonians and for
those who believe that the states are bound to wither
away—there can be little attraction in revenue
sharing or other instruments relying heavily on local
discretion and decision.

Yet, apart from the philosophic virtues of federalism, all of us have a direct stake in the financial
health of state-local governments for the simple
reason that they perform the bulk of essential civilian
services in the country.

There is enough money at the center—i.e., in our
federal government—to *finance* our national programs, but there is not enough wisdom to *admin-*

ister them centrally. So we rely heavily on states and localities as service stations to carry out the centrally financed functions. If those service stations are weak and undermanned, if the state-local junior partners are too junior, the national programs are bound to "suffer in the translation."[8]

- A great many of the seemingly humdrum services provided by state-local governments on their own account, with little or no federal help, form an integral part of the base for the good and great society we seek. Police protection and law enforcement, sanitation, recreation facilities, street maintenance and lighting—things that, together with housing and schooling, spell the difference between a decent and a squalid environment, a respectable neighborhood and an explosive ghetto —are cases in point. We neglect them at our peril.

Tax sharing and state-local vitality. Tax sharing would respond to these considerations in several different ways:

a) by providing new financial elbow-room, free of fatal political penalties, for innovative and expansion-minded state-local officials, i.e., by serving our federalist interest in vitality and independence at the state-local level;

---

[8] One rough-and-ready indicator of the existing imbalance is provided by the unweighted average weekly earnings of federal and state employees (other than in education) in 1965: $131.71 for federal employees and $103.27 for state employees. (U.S. Bureau of the Census, *Public Employment in 1965*, pp. 12–17.)

b) by nourishing the purely local services and building up the staff and structure needed to carry out effectively the national-interest or spillover type of services financed by categorical aid, i.e., by serving the universal interest in competence and efficiency;

c) by enabling the economically weaker states to provide the same scope and quality of services as their wealthier brethren without putting crushingly heavier burdens on their citizens, i.e., by serving the national interest in reducing inter-state disparities in levels of services associated with any given tax effort.

A moment's reflection will show that grants-in-aid are not meeting these needs. Though they admirably serve the national purpose, they often put state-local finance at cross-purposes. In drawing on a limited supply of resources to finance and staff particular functions, the matching grant tends to siphon re-sources away from the non-aided programs. The poorer the state, the greater the tax effort that must be made to achieve any given amount of matching, and hence the less that is left over for the purely state-local functions. To some extent, then, the state-local government trades fiscal freedom for fiscal strength.

In contrast, revenue-sharing or similar general-purpose grants would combine freedom with strength. On the one hand, the funds would not be tied to spec-ified national interests, bound by detailed controls, forced into particular channels and subject to annual federal decisions. On the other, it would not have to be wrung out of a reluctant state-local tax base at great political risk to bold and innovative governors and legislators. In short, revenue sharing would provide a dependable flow of federal funds in a form that would enlarge, not restrict, the options of the state and local decision-makers.

One readily visualizes the tangible benefits: higher salaries and hence higher caliber staffs; better performance of the jobs the federal government subcontracts to states and localities; and a more effective attack on problems beyond the reach of federal projects and the present system of federal aids.

The intangible gains are even more promising. General-assistance grants would offer some relief from the intensive fiscal pressures that lead local governments to default to the states, and state governments to default to Washington; would help the nation tap not only the skills and knowledge but the wisdom and ingenuity of our state and local units; and would enable these units to flex their muscles and exercise greater discretion and responsibility.

Yet, in appraising the net impact of tax sharing on state-local vitality, one cannot ignore the fears of the critics that gains on this front will either be thwarted or nullified by two major offsetting factors:

- First, it is feared that turning revenues over to the states without federal controls would sacrifice national priorities, would divert funds from high-priority education, urban renewal, and poverty programs to low-priority uses.
- Second, critics in this conference and elsewhere

charge that state-local government is so often inefficient, wasteful, and corrupt that it is unworthy
of anything but tightly controlled federal support.

National priorities. Underlying the fear that revenue sharing would undercut national programs is the
assumption that it would drain funds away from
these programs rather than slow down the longer-
term process of federal income tax reduction. But
the alternative assumption is just as reasonable, if
not more so. Revenue sharing would convert the
two-way tug-of-war between expenditures and tax
reductions into a three-cornered competition for
funds. And especially if the state-local share were
clearly earmarked as a direct federal collection on
behalf of states and localities and channeled to them
through a trust fund, its status as a direct competitor
with tax cuts would be underscored.

This point is reinforced by the strength of the
budgetary push behind federal civilian programs.
The defenders of these programs have some impres-
sive advantages in the battle for funds. Federal organization, whether in the executive agencies, in the
budget process, or in the Congressional committees
is largely along functional lines. Private interest
groups and pressures operate along the same lines.
Speak of schools, highways, farm subsidies, or health
programs—and groups in the Administration, Congress, and private life spring to the colors and man
the budgetary battle stations. This is not to say that
these programs have things all their own way—wars
on poverty and urban squalor, for example, command weaker legions—but it does suggest that most

of them can hold their own in the three-cornered battle of the budget. To the extent that they can, it follows that revenue sharing would compete primarily with tax cuts and that the net effect would be to route more funds into the public sector.

And in speaking of priorities, one should note three further points:

· As already noted, some of the prosaic functions of states and localities come pretty close to the heart of our national purpose.
· In deploying $37 billion of increased expenditures between 1954 and 1964, states and localities assigned 41 per cent to education, and another 14 per cent to health and welfare. It is hard to fault them on this order of priorities.
· It is by no means clear that our present system of conditional aids, given its highly fragmented nature and its matching provisions, achieves the right order of priorities. The suction of the matching requirements sometimes draws funds away from non-aided functions that represent higher-priority, and hence more efficient, uses. Flanking our system of tightly tied aids by wide-latitude grants of the type represented by revenue sharing is, in fact, necessary to achieve an optimum allocation of state-local funds.

Inefficiency and waste. In its crudest form, the charge here is that the state-local vessels into which federal funds would be poured are cracked and leaky. State legislatures are said to be dominated by corrupt and interest-ridden buccaneers. State adminis-

trations are said to be weak and incompetent. Local governments are said to be hopelessly archaic in management and structure.

No doubt one could find horrible examples to fit each of these charges, and one can readily grant that state-local government has not done nearly enough to overcome obsolete and ineffective administration. But one must also be careful not to condemn by cliché. Not only does reapportionment promise fairer and more intelligent allocation of funds, but the picture of administrative competence is greatly overdrawn. After mingling with governors and their staffs at the National Governors' Conference, one observer put it this way:

The great majority of the Governors . . . are dedicated, hard-working, and above all, highly competent individuals, handling complex administrative and policy problems that would overwhelm many a Senator.
. . . for the most part, too, these men are surrounded by trained, talented, staffs, not mere political cronies and hangers-on.[9]

One might add, in answering the critics, that it is precisely to enable the states to overcome some of their weaknesses that broad-gauged grants are so badly needed. Denying the state such assistance would perpetuate those evils that are not simply in the eyes of the beholders.

Beyond the point that the vessels are alleged to be cracked and leaky, it is claimed that moneys flowing in without the pain and suffering of self-

---

[9] Alan L. Otten, "Governors Make Good Impression," *Wall Street Journal,* July 30, 1965.

taxation or the penalty of federal controls would be spent like water. Yet it is difficult to see why the proposed sharing of revenues with the states would promote loose spending:

- The federal funds, unmarked by any radioactive tracers, would be commingled with state and local funds.
- They would cover only a modest per cent of the cost of any given program; the bulk of the funds would be the community's own hard-earned tax money.
- Since the flow of receipts each year would be fixed, there would be none of the incentive to profligacy that arises when the spender knows that "there's always more where that came from."

Perhaps one also has to deal with the specious but persistent charge that revenue sharing would be costly because of "the additional freight of a round trip to Washington." This charge flies in the face of three plain facts:

- Costs of collecting federal taxes, per dollar of revenue, are far below costs of collecting state local taxes.
- Given its advantages in jurisdiction, size, and scale, the Internal Revenue Service is an inherently more efficient tax administering agency than those of the states.
- With respect to plans like revenue sharing, there would need to be no new machinery and no added administrative costs of any consequence; the round trip to Washington would cost less than a round trip to the State House or City Hall.

24

Walter W. Heller

Impact on Inequality, Income Distribution, and Tax Effort

Interstate equalization. A significant part of the case for revenue sharing rests on its role in narrowing the gaps in service levels between wealthier and poorer states. Those gaps are huge. For example, in 1964 the total state-local expenditures per capita ranged from $512 in the highest five states to $252 in the lowest five. For education, the range was $197 to $94. For public welfare, it was from $52 to $15.[10]

The story for per capita revenue collections is much the same. The five top states (New York, Nevada, California, Wyoming, and Washington) collected $396 per capita in 1964, or roughly twice the $197 per capita collected in the five bottom states (South Carolina, Arkansas, Mississippi, Alabama, and Kentucky). Yet the tax effort in the poor states matches that in the rich. The most recent figures show that the ten richest states realize their revenue bounties with just about the same tax burden—as a percentage of personal income—as the ten poorest states.[11]

The inescapable conclusion that the poorest states are making just as great a tax effort as the richest states—and getting a much poorer diet of governmental services for their pains—is a serious indictment of the workings of our fiscal federalism.

Revenue sharing on a per capita basis alone would have a significant interstate equalizing effect. As

[10] U.S. Bureau of the Census, *Governmental Finances in 1964.*
[11] Joseph A. Pechman, *Federal Tax Policy* (Brookings Institution, 1966), pp. 207–8.

already noted, at 2 per cent of the individual income tax base in 1967, the allocation would be $30 per capita to all of the states. Yet the 2 per cent would draw about $42 per capita from the ten richest states and $18 from the ten poorest.

One should note in passing that this points up the difference between per capita revenue sharing and sharing on the basis of origin, i.e., returning revenues to the point of collection (as proposed in many of the tax-sharing bills now before Congress). The latter would return the same $42 to the richest states and $18 to the poorest states that came from those respective states. One should also note here that on this count, the federal crediting device—credits against federal income tax for state income taxes paid—is similar to sharing income tax on the basis of origin.

Going beyond the per capita formula by reserving 10 per cent of the total funds for distribution to the lowest-income third of the states—as Pechman and I advocate—would raise the grants to those states by 70 per cent. The easy adaptability of revenue-sharing plans to almost any preference as to equalization among the states can be an important asset.

Distribution of fiscal burdens. In recent years sharp increases in state-local taxes (four-fifths of which were derived from property, sales, and gross receipts taxes) coupled with sharp reductions in federal income tax rates and increases in social security payroll taxes have moved our federal-state-local tax system in a regressive direction. Carried to extremes, this would find us dismantling the progressive federal income tax and leaning ever more heavily upon regressive state-local property, sales, and excise taxes. Most of us would accept, as an article of faith, that we should halt this trend and seek instead a system in which the powerful federal income tax is used to support expenditures which otherwise either could not be made at all, or would have to be financed from regressive tax sources.

As already indicated, it seems politically realistic to assume that the revenue shares put aside for the states would absorb funds that would otherwise have gone mainly into federal income tax reduction and only partly into expenditure increases. It would transform them mainly into increases in state-local expenditures and partly into a slow-down of state-local tax increases. In either case, the combination would contribute to the progressivity of our over-all fiscal system.

Facing an increase of 7 to 8 per cent per year in their expenditure demands, not many state and local governments would channel their fiscal dividends from the federal government into tax reduction. No doubt, revenue sharing would slow down their increases in sales, property, and excise taxes and lead to an occasional cut in such taxes.[12] But slowing down the reduction of our federal individual income tax in order to relieve pressures on regressive, inequitable, and inefficient property and consumer taxes is hardly what I would label original fiscal sin. It would increase the progressivity of the tax sys-

---

[12] Richard P. Nathan, paper dealing with the potential impact of general aid in four selected states (prepared for the Committee for Economic Development; to be published shortly).

tem and shift burdens away from taxes that bear most unevenly on consumers and business costs.[13]

Full use of the shared revenue for higher state-local expenditures would, of course, have an even more progressive effect since their benefits are heavily weighted toward the lower-income groups. True, the ratio of federal expenditures to income drops as income rises: from 42 per cent of the poorest incomes to 17 per cent of incomes over $10,000. But the state-local ratio declines far more sharply and steadily—from an estimated 43 per cent of income for the poorest families to 6 per cent for families with incomes of $10,000.

Study after study has confirmed the unmistakable pattern of substantially progressive federal taxes and expenditures, strongly regressive state-local taxes, and strongly progressive state-local expenditures. Such studies settle no questions of social priority or efficiency in taxing and spending. But they leave no doubt that a shift of federal income tax revenues to the states and localities would make our over-all fiscal system more progressive.

Tax effort and income tax credits. To say that the distributive implications of some let-up in state-local fiscal effort would not be unfavorable is not to say

---

[13] W. I. Gillespie and R. A. Musgrave in R. A. Musgrave (ed.), *Essays in Fiscal Federalism* (Brookings Institution, 1965), show that while state-local tax burdens rise gently with income in the lowest income brackets—from 12 per cent of income below $2,000 to 18 per cent in the $4–5,000 income bracket—they then regress with a vengeance, dropping to 6 per cent on incomes of $10,000 and over. In contrast, federal tax burdens run from 18 per cent of family income below $2,000 to 31 per cent over $10,000.

that greater effort, and particularly greater equality of effort, should not be encouraged. As already noted, an effort index could easily be built into the revenue-sharing formula to reward the high-effort states and penalize the low-effort states. Without such an index, federal income tax credits would be clearly superior in stimulating state-local tax efforts.

In passing, I should make clear that federal income tax crediting is a highly attractive device, particularly if it can be coupled with tax sharing or general assistance. One cannot deny that the case of the states for a share in the federal income tax is weakened by the facts that, even after action in 1964 by Michigan and Nebraska, fifteen states are still without income taxes; that twelve states impose a tax that amounts to less than 1 per cent of federal adjusted gross income; that another twelve have income tax burdens under 2 per cent; that only nine have effective rates of over 2 per cent—ranging to a maximum of over 3 per cent in Delaware, Oregon, and Wisconsin.[14] A form of federal fiscal support which would lead the states into these green pastures of growth and progression that they are now so widely neglecting has an understandably strong attraction.

In the best of all worlds, one would hope to be able to afford both the income tax credit and revenue sharing. If a choice has to be made, the balance of advantages seems to favor the revenue-sharing plan:

---

[14] John Shannon, "Recent Developments on the State Personal Income Tax Front" (Advisory Commission on Intergovernmental Relations, November 1965).

—first, because of its contributions to interstate equalization;

—second, because its entire proceeds would flow into state and local treasuries while a good part of the benefits of the tax credit would initially accrue directly to the taxpayers rather than to their governments;

—third, because the tax credit would have to overcome the barriers involved in inducing (some would say, coercing) fifteen states to adopt a tax they have not chosen to adopt on their own.

Having said this, however, one must hasten to add that adoption of an income tax credit would be a major advance in federal-state fiscal relations, a very good second best to the tax sharing approach. Those of us who labor in the vineyards of federal-state fiscal relations should take care that the good becomes the handmaiden, not the enemy, of the best.

The Claims of the Cities

Per capita revenue sharing would miss its mark if it failed to relieve some of the intense fiscal pressures on local, and particularly urban, governments. Indeed, it is in and through the metropolitan area that most of our aspirations for a greater society will be achieved or thwarted. Revenue sharing cannot be expected to break the bottlenecks of tradition and vested interest that stand in our path. And one should always bear in mind that it will be a supplement to federal programs for model cities, for urban redevelopment, for community action against poverty, and the like. But both in concept and in practice, revenue sharing still has a vital role to play in strengthening urban finance.

The question before us is not *whether* revenue sharing should put funds at the disposal of local governments, but *how*. Can one count on relief coming automatically from a no-strings grant made to the states, or should a specific part of the state shares be reserved for the local units?

In resolving this question, one is torn between two conflicting considerations: On one hand, one fears— with good reason—that some states, left to their own devices, will be unwilling to share and share alike with their local units. On the other, one is reluctant to weigh the revenue-sharing plan down with so many complexities that it falls of its own weight, or so many conditions that it loses its character as a new instrument and becomes simply another form of categorical aid.

What one seeks, then, is an assured flow-through to needful local governments under simple rules. The simplest approach of all would be to leave it to the discretion of the states, and several considerations seem to point in this direction:

Flexibility. States differ greatly in their division of responsibility and finances between state and local governments. Some state governments finance as much as two-thirds of total state-local expenditures, while in other states they finance as little as one-third. Arrangements for state aids and locally shared taxes differ greatly, and the division of functional responsibilities between states and localities also varies quite markedly. Any federal sharing formula should allow for these variations.

Existing transfers. All states already give significant amounts of aid to local units. All told, transfers from state to local government account for about 30 per cent of local general revenues and about a third of state expenditures. In the fiscal year 1965, state aid to localities totaled over $14 billion, about $3 billion more than federal aids to state-local government.[15] We have little reason to fear, then, that the shared income tax revenues would simply be bottled up at the state level. Yet this is not to say that the implied pass-through of even a third of the shared revenues would be a fair share for local government, given the relentless demands pressing against its limited tax resources.

Reapportionment. One can expect reapportionment to improve intrastate allocations of funds. Undoubtedly, it will improve the urban-rural allocation. Yet even after reapportionment, central cities will be represented in proportion, not to their problems, but to their population. They cannot solve the crushing problems of poverty, racial disability, obsolete social capital, pollution, and undernourished public services from revenues drawn from their own limited tax bases.

In Chapter 3 of *New Dimensions*, I left open the issue of an explicit rule governing the pass-through to local governments. But in the light of urgent local needs, especially in urban areas—and observing the tendency of many state legislators to hew to more

---

[15] U.S. Bureau of the Census, *Government Finances in 1963–64,* p. 31.

generous service standards at the state than at the local level—I have been persuaded (in spite of the significant points made by Harvey Brazer in his discussion paper) that setting a minimum percentage pass-through is desirable to recognize the legitimate claims of local government.

I concluded my earlier discussion of the pass-through issue with the following equivocal statement: "How to give special weight to the claims of central cities and municipal areas, yet not freight the formula with too many conditions, remains a challenge to ingenuity."[16] Even though I have resolved my doubts in favor of *some* form of insurance of a pass-through, I, for one, cannot claim to have met the challenge. Formula after formula aimed at moving funds through the states to the most needful urban units shatters on the rocks of definition and complexity. Under formulas keyed to size, density, form of local unit—whatever the prescription—worthy claimants (needful local units) are left out in the cold, or unworthy ones are brought into the charmed circle, or both.[17]

---

[16] *New Dimensions*, pp. 161–62.

[17] One rather interesting approach would require each state to pass through to its municipalities and urban counties of 50,000 or more ("urban" being defined as involving at least 60 per cent of the population) a proportion of the state's allocation equaling the average of (1) the eligible governmental unit's tax revenue as a per cent of all state-local taxes in the state, and (2) the unit's population as a per cent of the total state population. In highly urban states, this formula would allocate a relatively large part of the states' allotments to the urban units, for example: California, 56 per cent; Illinois, 48 per cent; Maryland, 51 per cent; New York, 62 per cent. States would have no discretion on this portion of the pass-through, but would be free to

In determining state allotments, the basic formula could give extra weight to a high incidence of dependency, or urbanization, or poverty. But both as a matter of philosophy concerning the states' role in federalism and as a matter of administrative simplicity and flexibility in the face of sharply differing structures and problems of local governments in the fifty states, I am inclined to fall back on a simple percentage minimum or floor under the pass-through —with a preference for 50 per cent. This leaves the form and division of the localities' shares to the states' discretion.[18] This would put pressure on the states to recognize local needs while letting each state adapt the precise form and division of the local share to its particular pattern of local needs.

Possibly Congress could require the intrastate distribution to give weight to population and per capita income. And a joint council of responsible state and local officials might be required to assure a careful weighing of the general and special local needs in

---

supplement it if they wished. The special problem of over-allowance for some limited-activity county governments in New England might be met by setting a limit on the ratio of the pass-through allocation to the aided units' revenues from their own taxes. This example has been given to illustrate both the possible form of a mandatory pass-through for urban centers and some of the complex issues it raises, particularly the allocation of the urban share among city and suburbs and between component urban political jurisdictions within large metropolitan areas.

[18] Senator Javits meets the problem of a minimum pass-through by requiring the states to distribute to the local governments an equitable proportion of their allotments, the ratio in each state to be no less than the average of the state's distribution of its own revenues to local governments over the previous five years (S. 2619, Sec. 4[b], 89th Cong.).

each state. Even if these steps prove feasible, we would have to keep our fingers crossed in the hope that

—the minimum pass-through would not also become the maximum;
—states would not take refuge in the fungibility of funds by dutifully conforming to the pass-through requirements while simultaneously reducing other payments to their local governments;
—the federal government would sharply step up its wars on poverty, ignorance, blight, disease, and pollution that beset our beleaguered cities today.

This is not to say that it is impossible to devise a formula taking into account the several critical variables that measure and differentiate among the needs of different urban areas in the United States. But even if a satisfactory multivariate formula could be devised, it would leave unanswered a major question about a fixed formula pass-through (a question that the minimum percentage pass-through, which leaves the method of local distribution to the states, does not raise): Are we prepared, in effect, to bypass the states on this score and correspondingly enlarge the role of the cities in our federal system?

A major flow of unconditional federal funds directly to the cities would represent a basic realignment of powers in our federalism and should be recognized as such. I distinguish sharply here between conditional program aids to support particular functions with large spillover effects and direct general-purpose financing of the cities as such.

In the former, the case for direct federal intervention and support is clear, and the cities—like other state and local governments—play the role of service agents.[19] But in the latter, even if one observes the nicety of passing funds through the state's hands rather than dealing the cities a direct hand, the net effect is to cut away an important piece of the state's basic responsibility for state-local functions, structure, and financing.

One may argue that the nation will be forced to bypass and downgrade the states if they refuse to live up to their responsibilities, fail to modernize their structure and operations, and ignore or slight their cities' urgent needs. But this line of argument points to strengthening rather than weakening the states as units in our federal system. What practical alternatives do we have?

One may believe that regional governments, or regrouped states, or major metropolitan areas would be more effective repositories of decentralized power. But in the real world in which we live, it is fair to say that the states are here to stay. One may or may not agree with Paul Ylvisaker that "if the states did not exist, we would have to invent them." Yet, where one tries to visualize the cities with their limited tax sources going it alone—except for distant

---

[19] In the fiscal year 1968, an estimated $10.3 billion of federal conditional aid will be paid in urban areas, two-thirds through the states and one-third in the form of direct grants to local urban governments. (Selma Mushkin, "Issues in Federal Tax Sharing," a paper prepared for the U.S. Conference of Mayors, February 24, 1967, unpublished, p. 9.) Her paper contains an illuminating discussion of the problems and complexities involved in trying to devise a pass-through formula.

federal support—one wonders how long they could last as viable entities without "membership" in the states. And even more persuasive to believers in federalism who want to strengthen its decentralized base is the political reality that they will have to work with the existing fifty institutions known as states. There are no politically acceptable substitutes in sight.

The requirement of a minimum pass-through recognizes that the states are far from perfect, but avoids the declaration of urban independence from the states that would be implicit in direct federal shares to the cities. If the federal government were to go very far in the direction of defining what is or is not a bona fide local government and then financing it independently of the states, little more than state flowers and different colors on automobile license plates would be left to mark their erstwhile role in our federalism.

Conclusion

I have been making a general case in terms of a particular plan. But let me stress again that it is the general case, not the particular plan, that matters. The important thing is to be ready to move from talk to action once Vietnam relents—to harness federal funds to state-local initiative as part of the national undertaking to convert economic growth into a better life. The good life will not come, ready-made, from some federal assembly line. It has to be custom built, engaging the effort and imagination and resourcefulness of the community. Whatever fiscal plan is adopted must recognize this need.

The new plan will not be working alone. Reapportionment has already realigned most state legislatures. New demands flooding in on the states and localities are stirring new efforts at administrative and legislative reform. A growing sense of social corrosion and crisis—of which riots and fires in the urban ghettoes are explosive examples—is awakening a new sense of state and local responsibility. And sustained prosperity is opening new vistas of fiscal hope. In sum, new federal efforts to stiffen the state-local fiscal spine would be only one of several powerful forces already gathering for a renaissance of the states.

THE FEDERAL GOVERNMENT AND FEDERALISM

*Richard Ruggles**

Since the founding of the United States, the functions and interrelationships among the federal, state,
and local governments have been subject to a variety
of evolutionary forces which bear upon both the tax
systems available to the various levels of government and their programs of expenditures. Because
different forces bear on the tax systems and the expenditure programs of the different levels of government, there is no assurance that an optimum balance
will be struck, or that the total mix of government
activity with respect to either taxes or expenditure
will be ideal.

While the task of designing an ideal governmental
system may not be a feasible one, from time to time
the possibility may arise of making incremental
changes that will significantly alter the nature of the
system. There is strong evidence that options of this
kind may be available to us in the foreseeable future;
it will be useful, therefore, to consider their possible
range.

First, however, it will be necessary to examine the
role of government in the economy to see how the
importance of federal and state and local govern-

* Professor of Economics, Yale University.

ments has changed in relation to economic growth, and how the governments currently are fulfilling their different functions. After this brief review, the present dilemmas and possible alternative policies can be discussed.

A Review of Government Expenditures and Functions

The relative importance of federal, state, and local governments in the economy. In considering the relative importance of federal, state, and local governments in the economy, it is useful to ask four questions:

- How much of the total labor force is employed by each level of government?
- How much does each level of government take of the resources that are produced by the economy?
- How much do the various levels of government give away in the form of transfer payments, in addition to what they spend on goods and services?
- What is the relative size of the total budgets of the different levels of government (including the amount given by one level of government to another)?

Table 1 provides the information relating to these four questions for the period 1902 to 1965. The share of the labor force employed by all levels of government has risen since 1929 from about 6 per cent to over 15 per cent. The increase applies to every level of government, but is greatest in federal defense employment, which in 1965 accounted for almost 5 per cent of the total labor force. Federal

TABLE 1

Employment, Expenditures, and Budgets of Federal, State, and Local Governments

(Per cent)

Item	1902	1913	1929	1938	1950	1957	1965
Full-time equivalent employment as per cent of labor force:							
Federal defense	0.4	0.6	0.7	0.7	3.3	4.8	4.9
Federal non-defense	0.6	0.9	0.9	0.8	1.4	1.3	1.3
State	NA	NA	0.8	1.0	1.3	1.6	2.1
Local	NA	NA	3.7	3.9	4.1	4.9	6.1
Total	NA	NA	6.1	6.4	10.1	12.6	15.4
Expenditures on goods and services as per cent of gross national product:							
Federal defense	0.8	0.8	0.4	1.1	5.3	10.1	7.4
Federal non-defense	0.9	1.0	0.8	2.2	1.5	1.1	2.5
State	0.6	0.7	1.2	2.4	2.1	2.7	3.3
Local	4.5	4.7	5.7	6.4	4.8	5.5	6.9
Total	6.8	7.2	8.1	12.1	13.7	19.4	20.1
Expenditures on goods and services, subsidies, and transfers to individuals as per cent of gross national product:							
Federal defense	0.8	0.8	0.5	1.1	5.0	9.9	7.4
Federal non-defense	1.9	1.8	1.9	7.8	8.5	7.2	9.1
State	0.6	0.7	1.4	3.4	3.2	3.3	4.1
Local	4.6	4.8	6.1	7.5	5.0	6.0	7.2
Total	7.9	8.2	10.0	19.9	21.8	26.4	27.8
Total budgets (including intergovernmental transfers), per cent of total:							
Federal defense	9	9	6	5	19	33	23
Federal non-defense	24	21	24	37	36	27	33
State	11	12	17	23	21	17	20
Local	56	58	53	35	24	23	24
Total	100	100	100	100	100	100	100

Sources: U.S. Department of Commerce, *The National Income and Product Accounts of the United States, 1929–1965,* Supplement to the *Survey of Current Business* (1966); *Government Finances* (various); *Historical Statistics of the United States, Colonial Times to 1957* (1960).

non-defense employment, the least important, amounted in 1965 to approximately 1.3 per cent. Local governments employed 6 per cent of the total labor force, and since 1929 have accounted for about two-thirds of non-defense government employment— a circumstance that reflects the engagement of local governments in education, police, fire protection, and other local services that require substantial employment.

When the federal-state-local relationship is viewed in terms of the proportion of the total output of the economy each purchases, the patterns show some change. Since the turn of the century, governments of all levels have increased the goods and services they purchase from under 7 per cent of the gross national product to the present 20 per cent. The smallest increase was shown by local governments, which at the turn of the century accounted for more than two-thirds of total government expenditures, and now account for only one-third. Interestingly enough, although the proportion of total resources taken by federal and state governments has tripled since 1938, the proportion taken by local governments is very little higher today than it was thirty years ago. It is true that in 1938 there were 10 million unemployed and local expenditures were relatively high. However, much of the apparent rapid growth of local government during the 1950's is due to the fact that immediately after World War II local government expenditures were abnormally low.

When transfer payments and subsidies are taken into account, the relative importance of the different levels of government again changes. Prior to the 1930's the only significant transfer payments were those made to veterans. At the federal level these accounted for a sizable proportion of the non-defense outlays—approximately half. During the 1930's, transfer payments for relief (including work relief) became important, and at the federal level accounted for two-thirds of the non-defense budget. Transfers were less dominant at the state and local levels, although in both instances they became a major budget item. After World War II the situation changed dramatically. With social security, federal transfer payments for non-defense purposes became larger than those of any other level of government. This is in marked contrast to its role as an employer or purchaser of goods and services for non-defense purposes. In contrast, transfer payments are very much less important in the state government budgets, and for local governments transfers do not constitute a significant outlay.

Intergovernmental transfers are an important aspect also of the federal-state-local relationship. Categorical grants-in-aid, particularly in connection with highway transportation and public assistance, are given by the federal government to the state governments as a means of sharing costs and providing transfer payments. Similarly, states make grants to local governments to assist in providing such services as education, health, and public assistance.

Examination of total budgets at each level of government shows how their relative importance has changed since 1900. Initially, local budgets represented over half of the total budgets of all levels of government. In 1965, they represented less than a quarter—a share roughly equal to federal outlays for national defense. Federal non-defense outlays constitute approximately one-third of the total, and state outlays the remaining 20 per cent; approximately a quarter of state budgets is supplied by grants-in-aid from the federal government.

The functions of federal, state, and local governments. The different functions of federal, state, and local governments are directly reflected by their patterns of expenditure. These are shown for the years 1957 and 1965 in Table 2. Federal grants-in-aid to state and local governments are treated in this context as outlays by the federal government, and not as expenditures by state and local governments. Similarly, state grants to local communities are omitted from

TABLE 2
Government Expenditures by Type of Function, 1957 and 1965
(Billion dollars)

	1957			1965		
Function	Federal	State and local	Total	Federal	State and local	Total
1. Defense and international affairs	47.1	*	47.1	54.5	*	54.5
2. Administration	1.9	3.7	5.6	4.1	8.2	12.2
3. Economic development	6.0	7.4	13.4	18.4	9.8	28.2
Space	—	—	—	5.6	*	5.6
Transportation	1.9	6.3	8.2	5.4	7.6	13.0
Agriculture	2.3	0.4	2.6	4.4	0.6	5.0
Natural resources	1.1	0.4	1.5	1.9	0.5	2.4
Postal	0.6	—	0.6	0.8	—	0.8
Utilities	—	0.1	0.1	—	0.4	0.4
Other	0.1	0.3	0.5	0.4	0.6	1.0

4. Social development	3.3	18.2	21.4	6.9	34.5	41.4
Elementary and secondary schools	}0.3	11.5	}13.5	0.4	22.2	22.6
Higher education		1.8		0.4	4.6	5.0
Other education	0.9	0.5	1.6	0.4	1.3	1.8
Hospitals and sanitation	1.3	4.5	5.8	2.5	7.1	9.7
Housing and community development	*	*	*	0.6	−0.1	0.5
Other	0.8	0.1	0.7	2.3	−0.7	1.7
5. Community services	0.1	3.4	3.5	0.2	6.3	6.5
Police and correction	*	2.0	2.1	0.1	3.7	3.8
Fire	—	0.8	0.8	—	1.4	1.4
Recreation	0.1	0.6	0.6	0.2	1.2	1.3
6. Transfers to persons	15.5	2.0	17.5	30.9	3.2	34.1
Public assistance	1.7	1.9	3.6	3.4	3.2	6.6
Unemployment	1.8	—	1.8	2.3	—	2.3
Old age and retirement	8.2	—	8.2	19.7	—	19.7
Veterans	3.6	0.1	3.6	5.4	—	5.4
Other	0.2	—	0.2	0.2	—	0.2
7. Interest on debt	5.7	0.5	6.2	8.3	0.6	8.9
Total Expenditures	79.6	35.3	114.9	123.4	62.5	185.8

* Less than $50 million.

Note: Detail may not add to totals because of rounding. Negative amounts in state and local columns indicate that grants-in-aid received exceeded expenditures.

Source: U.S. Department of Commerce, *The National Income and Product Accounts of the United States, 1929–1965,* Supplement to *The Survey of Current Business* (1966).

local expenditures. Thus, each of the seven categories shows net state and local expenditures. Each of them, also, shows those programs which were the major objects of expenditure.

As is indicated in Table 1, defense and related expenditures are an important part of federal outlays and are negligible for state and local governments. In 1957 they accounted for almost 60 per cent of federal government outlays, but by 1965 had dropped to about 45 per cent. The relative decline resulted from a much slower growth of the federal government's defense expenditures than of the rest of its outlays. By now, of course, increased activity in Vietnam has caused a reversal in this trend.

With respect to administration, the federal government spent approximately half the amount spent in this category by state and local governments. While to some extent differences in accounting practices and classification procedures may be reflected here, it should be remembered that there are 90,000 state and local governments and that, as noted in Table 1, they employ six times as many people as the federal government. By their very nature, state and local governments are involved in providing services that require a substantial amount of administration.

In the area of economic development, the federal government now has more extensive programs than state and local governments. For long it has played a major role in agriculture, natural resources, and conservation. More recently, research and development in the field of space and space exploration has also absorbed a substantial amount of federal funds. The major expenditures of state and local governments in economic development relate to streets and highways. In more recent years this responsibility has been shared with the federal government through the grants-in-aid program designed to develop an interstate highway system.

Social development expenditures in 1957 were largely the responsibility of state and local governments. To some extent the federal government was involved in supporting hospitals (mainly for veterans), but state and local governments provided the support for public education and most of the public support for hospitals. By 1965, educational expenditures had doubled at the state and local level, absorbing over a third of their total budgets. The federal government still had made no significant expenditures in this area, but in other social areas it was taking on new responsibilities. Expenditures on health and hospitals increased substantially, and other social development expenditures by the federal government increased from an insignificant level to over $2 billion. When the expenditures for such new federal programs as Medicare and education are included for 1966 and later years, the role of the federal government in social development will be further increased.

Community services, mainly a local government function, take about 10 per cent of the total state and local budgets. The federal government's role in this area is confined to demonstration projects, experimental programs, etc., designed to improve the quality and efficiency of community services.

Transfers to persons are dominated by the old-age and retirement payments of the federal government, but, in addition, a substantial amount of other transfer payments are made: state and local transfer payments amount to close to 10 per cent of those provided by the federal government.

In summary, federal government functions, as shown by allocation of outlays, are those of national defense, economic development, and transfer payments to individuals. To an increasing extent, however, the federal government is entering the field of social development, particularly for education and health. State and local functions relate to social development and community services, although some economic development expenditures in the form of highway construction are shared with the federal government.

The Fiscal Crisis of State and Local Governments

Much of the concern about the present state of affairs arises from the feeling that state and local governments now face a fiscal crisis because their revenues are sluggish and their needs for expenditure are expanding at a fast rate. The fact that over recent years state and local governments have shown a surplus is, of course, no refutation of this argument; these governments are for the most part forced to live within their incomes, either by constitutional provisions or limits to their borrowing capacity, so that on balance a surplus will tend to result. As Heller[1] has pointed out, the fiscal crisis is more likely to be reflected in the fact that, due to inadequate financing, state and local governments cannot carry out their proper functions.

Although looking at the past performance of state and local revenues and expenditures will not reveal the extent to which they have failed to meet their proper obligations, it can show how their different elements have behaved and how the future pattern

---

[1] Walter W. Heller, *New Dimensions of Political Economy* (Harvard University Press, 1966).

may be expected to change. Table 3 presents these data for the periods 1955, 1960, and 1965. In this presentation, federal grants-in-aid are listed as a revenue item and are also included in the appropriate expenditure categories.

The rates of growth of receipts of state and local governments exceeded those of their expenditures in both the 1955–60 and the 1960–65 periods. Paradoxically, receipts increased faster (by an average of 10.2 per cent per year) in the 1955–60 period when gross national product grew only 4.8 per cent a year, than they did in the 1960–65 period when total receipts grew by 8.8 per cent and gross national product by 6.2 per cent per year. In both periods, however, almost all categories of receipts grew faster than the gross national product. Although this is also true for most categories of expenditures in the period 1955–60, the rate of growth in health, transportation, and public assistance was only equal to or less than the growth in gross national product. It should be recognized, of course, that growth in tax receipts at the state and local level was not automatic. Mushkin and Lupo[2] have estimated that over the period in question effective tax rates increased by approximately 2 per cent a year. Furthermore, a continual revaluation for assessment purposes is required to prevent effective property tax rates from dropping when the market value of property increases.

A number of different projections have been made

---

[2] Selma J. Mushkin and Gabrielle C. Lupo, "Project '70: Projecting the State-Local Sector," The George Washington University, State-Local Finances Project, p. 33.

TABLE 3

Receipts and Expenditures of State and Local Governments,
1955–65, and Rates of Growth, 1955–60–1965–70

Item	Receipts and expenditures (*billion dollars*)			Annual percentage rates of growth		
	1955	1960	1965	1955–60	1960–65	1965–70[a]
Gross national product	397.5	502.6	681.8	4.8	6.3	4.8
Personal tax and non-tax receipts	4.2	7.3	11.8	11.7	11.5	7.0
Income taxes	1.4	2.7	4.4	14.0	10.3	—
Motor vehicle taxes	0.5	0.8	1.0	9.9	4.5	—
Other	2.3	3.8	6.4	10.6	10.8	—
Corporate profits tax accruals	1.0	1.3	2.0	5.4	9.0	6.2
Indirect business tax and non-tax accruals	21.8	32.5	45.8	8.3	7.1	6.1
General sales taxes	3.7	5.8	8.7	9.4	8.4	—
Gasoline, tobacco, liquor	3.4	5.1	7.1	8.4	6.8	—
Property taxes	10.4	16.1	23.1	9.6	7.5	—
Other	4.3	5.5	6.8	5.0	4.3	—
Contributions for social insurance	1.7	3.0	4.5	12.0	8.4	5.6
Federal grants-in-aid	3.0	6.3	11.2	16.0	12.2	13.1
Surplus of government enterprises	1.6	2.2	3.2	6.6	7.8	8.7
Total receipts	33.3	51.6	78.6	10.2	8.8	7.4
Purchases of goods and services	30.3	46.5	69.4	8.9	8.3	7.5
General administration	3.6	6.2	8.2	11.5	5.7	6.3
Education	11.4	17.8	28.9	9.3	10.2	8.5
Health and sanitation	3.7	5.6	7.6	8.6	6.3	7.5
Police and fire	2.4	3.5	5.1	3.8	7.8	5.6
Transportation	6.0	8.5	11.5	7.2	6.2	7.8
Other	3.2	4.9	8.3	8.9	11.1	—

Transfer payments to						
persons	3.5	5.0	6.9	7.4	6.7	3.5
Public assistance	2.6	3.4	4.2	5.5	4.3	6.8
Other	0.9	1.6	2.7	12.2	11.0	—
Net interest paid	0.5	0.7	0.6	7.0	−3.1	5.5
Total expenditures	34.3	52.2	76.9	8.9	8.1	7.1
Surplus or deficit	−1.0	+0.6	+1.7	—	—	—

[a] Projected by Mushkin and Lupo. See source below.

Sources: U.S. Department of Commerce, *The National Income and Product Accounts of the United States, 1929–1965,* Supplement to *The Survey of Current Business* (1966); Selma J. Mushkin and Gabrielle C. Lupo, "Project '70: Projecting the State-Local Sector," The George Washington University, State-Local Finances Project. (Summarized in *Review of Economics and Statistics,* Vol. 49 [May 1967].)

of both state and local revenues and expenditures. Pechman's prediction[3] of a fiscal crisis is predicated in part on his assumption that, at a minimum, state and local government expenditures will need to rise by 7 per cent a year in order to meet foreseeable needs and that future revenues cannot be expected to do much more than keep pace with the increase in gross national product, which he assumes to be 5 per cent a year. These figures lead, of course, to a substantial shortfall, resulting in a gap between revenue and needed expenditures of approximately $15 billion by the year 1970. In the absence of additional federal aid, Pechman indicates that state and local governments would have to raise their taxes, but he feels that this is unlikely to occur.

---

[3] Joseph A. Pechman, "Financing State and Local Government," in American Bankers Association, *Proceedings of a Symposium on Federal Taxation,* 1965, p. 76; also published as Reprint No. 103, Brookings Institution, 1965.

Other estimates by Netzer[4] and Mushkin and Lupo[5] come out with a somewhat higher level of revenue needs and differ somewhat in their estimates of the availability of revenue. The Mushkin and Lupo estimates suggest that the 1970 gross additional fund requirements are within the borrowing capacity of states and localities. The projections of expenditure must, of course, by their very nature involve many assumptions, but the estimates, detailed state by state and category by category, developed by "Project '70" do take many important factors into account which more aggregative analyses might well omit. Thus, for example, the projection of education expenditures is based on population data indicating the number of children who will be enrolled at various levels of school. Change in educational costs and the expected improvement of quality standards has also been estimated. The projections of revenue involve the examination of such elements as the expected change in the market value of real property related to changes in the level of gross national product, as reflected in past experience. The elasticity of sales and other gross receipts taxes is similarly estimated. As a result of these projections, Mushkin and Lupo concluded that the yearly increase in tax receipts would exceed 7 per cent over the period 1964–70. The results of the Mushkin-Lupo projections, by general category of

---

[4] Dick Netzer, "State-Local Finance in the Next Decade" (unpublished manuscript prepared for the Committee for Economic Development, August 1965), cited in Heller, *New Dimensions.*

[5] "Project '70," p. 46.

receipts and expenditures, are shown in the final column of Table 3. The figures presented here differ somewhat from those contained in the original study, since data through 1965 are now available, and the growth rate of the gross national product in the last two years has exceeded the rate of 5.7 per cent a year which was assumed in the original study.

Tax effort of state and local governments and the fiscal crisis. If there is a fiscal crisis, it would suggest that in those states where needs are the greatest the tax effort is near its maximum level. In considering this question, Pechman[6] ranks the states by the size of their per capita personal income, and shows state and local revenues as a percentage of personal income for each quintile of the distribution. These results are given below.

Quintiles of States Arranged by State Per Capita Income	Revenues as Per Cent of Personal Income
1 (lowest per capita income)	12.8
2	13.9
3	13.5
4	13.0
5 (highest per capita income)	12.0

Although these figures do suggest, as Pechman indicates, that poorer states may not be able to provide adequate levels of public services, the data in this form obscure the variances in tax effort which actually do exist from state to state. In terms of taxes

[6] Joseph A. Pechman, *Federal Tax Policy* (Brookings Institution, 1966), pp. 207–8.

collected rather than revenue (which includes charges and other receipts), the variation runs from a low of 8.1 per cent of personal income to a high of 12.7 per cent. Furthermore, there does not seem to be any outstanding pattern suggesting that it is the poor states which are putting forth maximum tax effort. The table below shows the data for the five lowest and the five highest states:

Tax Collections as a Percentage of Personal Income

Alaska	8.1	Minnesota	12.7
Ohio	8.6	Vermont	12.7
Virginia	8.6	California	12.6
Montana	8.7	South Dakota	12.6
Illinois	8.9	Wisconsin	12.6

Perhaps an even more interesting question than that of total tax collection as a percentage of personal income is whether state and local governments are making best use of the tax sources traditionally available to them. Specifically, is the property tax, which provides the basis for many local government expenditures, equally well utilized by the different states? Here the differences are found to be even greater than those indicated above.

	Average Effective Property Tax Rate 1962 (per cent)	Current Expenditure per Pupil in Daily Attendance, 1966 ($)
New England	2.2	544
Middle Atlantic	2.3	732
East North Central	1.6	538
West North Central	1.5	515
South Atlantic	0.9	421
East South Central	0.7	354
West South Central	0.7	452
Mountain	0.8	511
Pacific	1.0	581
United States Average	1.4	532

These figures[7] show that the average effective property tax rate of the Middle Atlantic states was three times that found in the East South Central and West South Central states, and, furthermore, that expenditures on education per pupil were lowest in those regions where property taxes were lowest. If it is reasonable to expect that market values of property bear some relation to rates of return, it would appear that property owners in certain regions of the country are being taxed much more lightly than in other regions and that local governments in these areas may not be making the most effective use of property taxes which could be used to support a higher level of educational expenditures.

Whether or not a fiscal crisis at the state and local government level does exist, the true fiscal duress, according to Heller, should be measured by the "unmet needs for school facilities, sewers, sidewalks, street lights, green space, more frequent garbage and trash collection," or by "rutted streets, crumbling curbs, deteriorating parks, miserable housing in urban ghettoes, . . . poverty, delinquency, and crime." It is these major omissions which, in the view of many, point up the fact that the fiscal needs of states and local governments vastly exceed their available revenues.

In contrast, it is pointed out that the federal tax system has produced a very different situation. The federal income tax and the corporate profits tax gen-

---

[7] U.S. Bureau of the Census, special study, *Property Taxation*, 1962; and U.S. Department of Health, Education, and Welfare, Office of Education, *Fall 1965 Statistics of Public Schools*.

erate substantial revenue as the economy grows. This feature of the federal tax system led to the tax reduction of 1964, which was designed to lessen the drag of federal taxes on economic growth. It is admitted that the current needs of Vietnam may cause federal expenditures to rise faster than its revenue, but this situation is considered to be a temporary one, and we should be looking forward to the design of tax policy in the period after the Vietnam conflict is settled, when the rapid automatic growth of federal revenues will again outstrip the rise in federal expenditures.

Proposals for Federal Action

In view of the unsatisfactory situation with respect to state and local governmental functions and their financing, and the simultaneous expectation that in the future federal revenues may increase at a faster rate than federal expenditures, two specific proposals have been developed which are intended to help solve the fiscal problems of state and local governments. The first proposal is that the federal government should permit tax credits to be charged against the federal income tax, so that states may introduce or increase income taxes without causing an equivalent rise in the tax burden on the individual. The second proposal is that the federal government should allocate a portion of its tax revenue to provide unrestricted per capita grants to the individual states.

The proposals for federal tax credits. In 1966 the Advisory Commission on Intergovernmental Relations[8] proposed an income tax credit which would allow a taxpayer to credit against his federal income tax liability 40 per cent of the income tax payment which he made to his state. Currently, a taxpayer can deduct state income tax payments in computing his taxable income for federal income tax purposes. For those individuals who pay less than a marginal rate of 40 per cent the tax credit would result in a tax saving, and it is reasoned that states, realizing this situation, could therefore increase their own tax rates without causing an additional burden to the taxpayer. For taxpayers who are paying a marginal rate in excess of 40 per cent, the present system of deductibility would be retained. It is argued that the tax credit will stimulate states that currently do not have an income tax to levy one, since the tax credit will yield a state additional revenue only if it takes advantage of the situation by introducing a state income tax or by increasing the rate of an existing tax. Thus the tax credit would cause a substitution of income taxes for the more regressive sales and property taxes more commonly in use, and would yield additional tax revenue to states without proportionally burdening the taxpayer.

One of the major criticisms of the federal tax credit plan is that additional revenue will be provided to states if, and only if, they are willing to take advantage of it by raising the rates of existing state income taxes or by instituting a state income tax if none exists. Unfortunately, it cannot be ex-

---

[8] ACIR, *Federal-State Coordination of Personal Income Taxes* (Washington, 1966).

pected that all states would take advantage of the federal crediting device. At present, over one-third of the states have no income tax, and some have constitutional provisions prohibiting such taxes.

The states standing to gain the most from a federal tax credit are the wealthy states where federal income tax collections are substantial. If states did not take full advantage in siphoning off all possible revenue, the benefits would accrue to those individual taxpayers who are currently paying the higher levels of taxes.

The federal tax credit plan provides for no equalization of income among states. It merely returns to the state a portion of the taxes which its citizens formerly paid to the federal government. The use of the tax credit device, therefore, does nothing about the disparity between the levels of income in the different states and the magnitude of their needs.

The nature of federal revenue sharing. The federal income tax revenue-sharing proposal put forth by Walter Heller and Joseph Pechman[9] is substantially different from the tax credit proposal and introduces a number of new features. Under the Heller-Pechman plan, the federal government would each year set aside for distribution to the states revenue equivalent to about 10 per cent of total federal personal income tax collections. However, the amount would be based on a fixed percentage of net taxable income, rather than revenue, in order to make it independent

---

[9] Heller, *New Dimensions;* Pechman, "Financing State and Local Government."

of the level and structure of federal tax rates and stabilization policies. The amount so derived would be set aside in a trust fund which would be used for periodic distributions to the states. This would emphasize the fact that the states would receive the funds as a matter of right, independently from annual Congressional appropriations and the regular budget process. In this respect it would resemble a sharing of revenue rather than a grant. The funds would be disbursed to the states on the basis of population.

Heller gives a well-reasoned and balanced discussion of the possible criticisms of revenue sharing and what might be done to meet these criticisms. The questions he examines are (1) the redistribution of income between states, (2) the possible effect on the tax effort of states, (3) whether the states would provide a pass-through of funds to local governments, (4) the allocation of funds to non-essential expenditures, and (5) the efficiency with which funds would be spent by state and local governments. Understandably, Heller is reluctant to encumber revenue sharing by attaching strings or adding complications, but he does, nevertheless, consider a number of different provisions.

With respect to the redistribution of income between states with low per capita income and those with high, Heller points out that the plan would provide a modest redistribution since the wealthier states do pay a heavier tax in per capita terms. If such limited redistribution is felt to be insufficient, Heller suggests that additional redistribution could be obtained by setting aside 10 to 20 per cent of the total funds to provide for additional grants to the states with a high incidence of poverty, dependency, or urbanization.[10]

With respect to tax effort, the charge has been made that providing states with unrestricted grants will enable them to reduce their own tax effort, or in any case that it will reduce the pressure to improve the equity and efficiency of their tax systems on states that are now slack in providing revenue. Heller does not consider this question at length, but he does indicate that it would be possible to stipulate that shares of those states which lowered their fiscal efforts would be reduced.[11] However, as has been discussed above, the problem of measuring tax effort raises many questions, and it may be difficult to take into account the wide differences in the tax efforts of local communities.

The problem of whether states will pass through enough of the funds to local governments (especially in urban areas) does disturb Heller. He believes that reapportionment will ease some of the difficulties; in his paper he suggests putting a floor under the pass-through by specifying that a minimum percentage (possibly 50 per cent) of the funds from revenue sharing should be earmarked for local governments. Such a provision, however, as Heller points out, would be easy to avoid, since any state wishing to retain the full amount of the grant would merely have to cut back on the amount of its existing grants to local governments; to freeze such grants would constitute federal interference with the decision-making process of the states.

---

[10] *New Dimensions*, p. 147.
[11] *Ibid.*

Wholly unrestricted grants create the possibility that they would be allocated by states for such undertakings as highway construction, which in turn could be used to obtain further federal funds. For this reason, Heller has suggested that perhaps the use of these funds might be restricted to such areas as health, education, and welfare,[12] but this restriction is similar to the restriction on pass-through; it cannot be operative as long as the revenue sharing constitutes a relatively small part of the total budget.

Finally, Heller responds to the criticism that administrative inefficiencies exist in the state and local governments by suggesting that reapportionment will provide better balance and new blood in legislatures, and that the charge of administrative incompetence is overdrawn.[13] This is, of course, a matter of faith, and one which is difficult either to prove or disprove. The answer which Pechman gives to this question is that in the past state and local governments have devoted a large part of the increase in their revenues to such essential services as education, health, and public assistance, and that therefore they would spend increased funds on urgently needed state and local services. This answer does not, however, indicate whether state and local governments have focused their expenditures *where* they are needed. Much of the problem within states is that substandard schools, hospitals, prisons, and blighted areas do exist alongside wealth. Much of the increase in state and local budgets can be dem-

---

[12] *Ibid.*
[13] *Ibid.*, p. 165.

onstrated to have gone to provide better facilities in areas where the level of facilities is already high, and problem areas are often given less than adequate attention.

Alternatives to Federal Tax Credits and Revenue Sharing

Both the federal tax credit plan and the revenue-sharing plan make the basic assumption that there is a sharp division between those programs which are federal in nature and those which are state and local. However, as the review of the past development of federal, state, and local functions has indicated, these relationships have been subject to major evolutionary changes. For example, the introduction of the social security system in the 1930's has had considerable impact on the 1960's. The county poorhouse for the aged is essentially a thing of the past. Today millions of aged are receiving as a matter of right a monthly social security check which supports them in their old age. More recently, the establishment of the Medicare program is also having a major impact on state and local support of health services for the aged. In effect, these federal programs are removing the problem of the aged population from the concern of state and local governments and have made it the concern of national policy administered by the federal government. It is not only that state and local governments were relieved of expenditures in this area; they were relieved of the major responsibility of providing for the minimum level of requirements of the aged population. Many states or communities may decide to supplement the health and

Richard Ruggles

other benefits afforded to the aged population, but such additional benefits are by their very nature a voluntary addition to existing programs rather than part of the basic minimum requirements.

In view of the actual changes that have occurred in the functions of the federal, state, and local governments over the past few decades, the basic premise of those advocating federal tax credits and federal revenue sharing should be questioned. Instead of suggesting that the federal government should provide state and local governments with additional resources, it may be more fruitful to ask whether or not some of the responsibilities that state and local governments are currently trying to meet are not in fact better performed by some other means. This should not mean merely the substitution of federal bureaucracy for state and local bureaucracy. The most desirable programs are those which, like the social security system, operate with a minimum of detailed administrative supervision and little need for arbitrary decision-making. Furthermore, in many cases, it may be possible for the federal government to provide the funding for operations that are carried out administratively by local units. With this in mind, it will be useful to examine those programs of state and local governments which currently account for the major part of their budgets and responsibilities. These are education, health, welfare, and urban problems.

Education. At the present time, the largest area of expenditures by state and local governments is education. In 1965 education absorbed $28 billion out of total state and local expenditures of approxi-

63

mately $62 billion. As in the case of social security
and health services, education is an important area
of social development which directly affects the income distribution and equality of opportunity of all
citizens. Poorer communities often cannot afford to
provide the basic minimum education required for
equal opportunity. Much of the current social fer-
ment relating to inadequate schools arises from the
difficulties of state and local governments in financing
education. To the extent that tax credits and revenue
sharing ease the fiscal situation of state and local
governments, it is undoubtedly true that some funds
would flow into the educational budgets. However,
there is no assurance that the funds would go to
those schools where the educational quality is lowest,
and where funds are most needed to provide equal
opportunity.

As an alternative approach, it would be possible
for the federal government to provide federal support
not to states but school boards directly, based on an
allowance per pupil in average daily attendance, so
that minimum resources for education would be provided to all schools.[14] This would not, of course,
prevent local communities from spending additional
amounts over and above the minimum as they de-
sired, financing this difference from their local or
state revenues just as they do at the present time.
For all communities this grant would provide sub-

---

[14] For an earlier proposal to establish a national "minimum
foundation program for education," see Alvin H. Hansen and
Harvey S. Perloff, *State and Local Finance in the National Economy* (W. W. Norton, 1944), pp. 145–51.

stantial additional revenues. If education expenditures had been below the amount required to provide an adequate minimum, the funds would be available and the necessary amount would have to be used to upgrade the education provided. Since even the least adequate school districts have been spending some funds on education, the federal grant would provide funds in excess of minimum requirements, thus enabling local governments to increase educational benefits over the minimum level, make other expenditures, or even reduce taxes. In communities where education was already above the minimum adequate level, the equivalent amount of the federal grant would be available for unrestricted use in exactly the same way as is proposed by the Heller-Pechman revenue-sharing plan. Insofar as states are now supplying funds to local communities for education, they, too, would be relieved of this burden, and could use the funds otherwise.

It is somewhat difficult to estimate precisely how much would be required to provide each elementary and secondary school with a per-pupil allowance for minimum adequate education. Average per-pupil expenditure for the country as a whole was $532 in 1966, and the range of state average expenditures varied from Mississippi at $317 to New York at $876. There are, of course, regional differences in costs, and within each state there is considerable variation among schools in the quality of education provided. The total cost of supporting a minimum education grant directly to school districts might run as high as a third to a half of the total amount spent on education at the elementary and secondary school level;

this would come to some $10 billion a year, and could be expected to increase.

If the program as a whole is too ambitious for the federal government to undertake all at once, it could be approached on a piecemeal basis; for instance, as in the Headstart Program, the federal government could underwrite first the first six grades of schooling, thereby cutting the cost of the program substantially. Or the federal government could contribute, say, 50 or 75 per cent of the cost of the minimum expenditure on education; this would at least provide sufficient funds to bring the less advantaged school districts up to a minimum adequate level.

With respect to higher education, it would also be possible for the federal government to provide funds on a per-student basis. Just as the Woodrow Wilson fellowships now provide funds both for the universities and for living allowances for the students, the per-student grant could carry with it a fixed amount intended to cover the institutional cost of providing him with education. This arrangement has the advantage of permitting students to choose their institutions of learning rather than forcing them to attend those which happen to receive federal and state funds and thus can provide a low tuition. In other words, per-student grants would provide both state and private institutions with a source of funds to cover costs.

Health. In the health field, it is clear that the Medicare program is having a substantial impact and will do much to provide support for both private and public hospitals. However, much still needs to be done. The difference in the level of quality among mental hospitals, for example, is quite striking, and in many states and communities the substandard facilities and services for mental patients are due to an inadequate provision of funds from state and local governments. Clinics and community health services are urgently needed as part of the program to improve health conditions in poverty areas. Federal support on a per-patient basis would be extremely useful in these areas.

Welfare. Insofar as welfare expenditures are concerned with the redistribution of income, the responsibility for them is, in fact, a national rather than a state and local responsibility. There has been considerable dissatisfaction with current proverty programs at all levels of government. The federal programs have been burdened with red tape and inefficiency, and the welfare programs of state and local governments have also been criticized. The long-run solution lies in ensuring that education and opportunity for coming generations are of such a nature that in the future there will be no large class of people who cannot support themselves adequately.

Even with the present generation of poor, policies aimed at increased self-sufficiency can be developed. Specifically, for example, day-care nurseries should be provided so that women who are mothers of dependent children and are also heads of households can take employment rather than subsist at home on welfare payments. Such a program of setting up day-care facilities in local communities should be an integral part of the attack on poverty and the redistribution of income, and as such should be supported by funds made available by the federal government.

Another action the federal government could take to relieve the need for public assistance is to develop some form of negative income tax. A major attraction of such a device, in both administrative and humanitarian terms, is that it avoids the costly and continuous case-by-case investigations by social workers of people whose incomes fall below the minimum level—a system degrading to the self-respect of those who are receiving public assistance. Where large poverty groups exist, a negative income tax based on objective and disinterested criteria could be a useful device since, properly handled, it would do its job without encouraging further dependence. The general problem of public assistance and poverty should be faced at the national rather than the state and local level because it involves the redistribution of income. If the burden is placed on local communities or states, the problem becomes greatest for the governments that are least equipped to handle it.

Urban problems. A number of programs at all levels of government deal with various kinds of urban problems. Many of them may involve several different but related communities, sometimes even neighboring states. Problems of air and water pollution, for example, which do not respect state boundaries, become difficult to handle on a single state or community basis. The recent effort of New York and New Jersey to co-operate on these problems is a case in point. At present, state and local governments spend little money in this area; the development of national policies and the provision of federal funds will relieve them of responsibilities that are administratively difficult and costly to fulfill.

The transportation problem represents another complex issue. Urban centers are becoming clogged with vehicular traffic, and further improvement of highways may only aggravate the situation. There is a growing realization that highways are intimately related to urban transport in general and to the development of metropolitan areas. High-speed transport systems between urban areas are also involved. The federal government's action in establishing the Department of Transportation constitutes a recognition of these interrelated problems.

The field of urban redevelopment and housing for lower-income groups has not so far received major funds from either the federal government or state and local governments. But, as in the case of transportation, this field is one in which future action will be required. Here a direct partnership between the federal government and urban communities might be a more suitable arrangement than passing the funds through the states, which would introduce additional administrative and political considerations. These have been underscored by the difficulties cities such as New York and Los Angeles have experienced in working with their state legislatures. The problem of urban redevelopment is indeed a difficult one; it requires careful consideration and planning over and above the outlay of huge amounts of funds.

In the field of community services, the role of the federal government is somewhat different. Normal outlays for police and fire protection and for recreation are properly the function of the local community. Just as we do not want a centrally administered educational system, so we do not want a centrally administered police force. The property tax available to local communities yields substantial revenues, and it seems quite proper that it should provide for the maintenance of law and order and the municipal services required for the operation of the community. To the extent that the federal government has any role at all with respect to community services, it is in terms of helping the individual communities by providing training centers for professional personnel, technical assistance, and research and development. If local communities have access to more qualified personnel, better methods, and improved equipment, they will be able to provide municipal services more efficiently. Police academies, communication equipment, and mechanization all can be drawn on by the local community if they are generally available.

The Role of Federal, State, and Local Government

In summary, it is clear that federal, state, and local governments perform very different functions, and it is important that these differences be recognized if there is to be fruitful co-operation between levels.

Besides providing for national defense, the federal government should be the instrument for developing national policy. Basically it is not an administrative unit, and so its administrative activities should be confined to the operation of well-defined systems such as the collection of taxes and the disbursement of social security funds and the funds for other programs that are chosen to be national programs. One of the major functions of the federal government should be to guarantee for every citizen access to an adequate level of education and health care. To the extent that redistribution of income is required in order to eradicate poverty, the federal government should be responsible. In such areas as transportation, air and water pollution, and natural resources, the federal government should, in co-operation with state and local governments, develop co-ordinated programs aimed at solving the associated problems. Care should be taken to see that the federal government does not develop monolithic programs in these areas, or become involved in highly detailed administrative and review procedures that are subject to arbitrary decisions. Rather, the federal government should encourage and provide funds for experimentation, research and development, and equal treatment of different groups wherever located.

States are basically regional governments. They provide an intermediate level of government between the single national government and the 90,000 local governments. A considerable part of their task is to oversee the local governments to discover whether they are in fact efficiently carrying out their functions; and, of course, they handle those matters which are of regional but not national importance.

Local governments provide required community services to the citizens. To the extent that the services relate to social development, such as education and health, local governments should be able to draw upon federal funds to help provide minimum adequate levels. They should be given freedom to administer these funds and to supplement these services as they desire by adding resources of their own, in much the same way that private firms supplement social security with private health and pension plans. Besides social development expenditures, communities should also provide basic community services such as police, fire, sanitation, and general city maintenance. It is quite proper that these services should be paid from local resources.

Such a division of functions between federal, state, and local governments would provide the individual citizen with a maximum amount of choice, and yet give him the assurance of adequate minimum services in the essential fields of social development and justice. The development over time will in great part depend on the development of our national standards with respect to the basic minimum requirements, and the extent to which different local communities find that they can afford and wish to exceed these standards by providing additional resources of their own. Federalism as a conscious division of functions between levels of government is a reasonable approach, but the encouragement of federalism through federal tax credits and revenue sharing constitutes an avoidance of the basic problems rather than an acceptable solution to them.

II

THE DISCUSSION

REFLECTIONS ON THE CASE FOR THE HELLER PLAN

Lyle C. Fitch[*]

My comments are addressed to what might be called the pure form of the "Heller plan"—a per capita block grant to states, with no conditions or restrictions. Heller, recognizing some of the weaknesses of the "pure form," has suggested some modifications. My own inclination is to go further and in a different direction. I suggest that any general-purpose federal grant should be used, not solely as a revenue-sharing measure, but also as a means of stimulating improvement in state and local government organization and planning.

Persuasive as I find Evangelist Heller, I am not quite ready to accept the pure gospel which calls for distributing the national dividend in the form of a per capita grant to states, with no conditions or restrictions.

The essence of the issue, it seems to me, is in the public decision-making processes of allocating resources and whether the state and local governments, *as now constituted*, are the best decision-makers we can command to dispose of the "national dividend." We have many alternative decision-makers to choose from, including the federal government, whose de-

* President, Institute of Public Administration.

cisions might call for direct expenditures or grants for specific purposes; taxpayers, whose decisions would be activated by tax reduction; the poor, assisted by some form of minimal income-guarantee program.

Certainly, state and local governments, beset by pressures of population growth and rising demands for services, need the money. Further, as HEW Secretary John Gardner has said: The problems of urban society are of such magnitude and are so diverse that it is increasingly difficult to deal with them by remote direction from Washington. What is needed is the development of greater local responsibility and people qualified to assume this responsibility.

Let us stipulate that the principal future concerns of domestic government will be posed by the measure of urban expansion—the U.S. urban population will increase by 75 to 100 per cent in the last third of the twentieth century. One implication is that we shall have to do more building—of housing, urban infrastructure and capital plant—between now and the end of the century than we have done in the past 350 years. And urban problems—the crawl of sprawl, traffic congestion, pollution, the shortage of recreation, the lagging response to housing needs—will increase in geometric proportion to population growth.

The crucial question is, who will determine the course of future urban expansion and set standards therefor? Thus far, most of the urban population growth has been accommodated by short-run market forces. The result is the specter of endlessly sprawling urban development reaching over hill and field, careless of efficiency, indifferent to beauty, heedless of any human values save the immediate need for a roof and four walls; holding out no aspirations or incentives for innovation in design, technology, or organization; paying little attention to efficient and harmonious spatial relationships between residence, employment, recreation, and activity centers.

But can adequate leadership be expected from the fifty states which would be the primary recipients of the federal largesse under the simple per capita grant plan and, beyond them, from the 90,000-odd local governments?

We should first consider Martin's observation that "only a few states have ever assumed significant program responsibilities in these areas. . . . The states have been slow to take meaningful hold of urban problems in the past, and there is little sign of any real intention to do so now."[1] The Advisory Commission on Intergovernmental Relations, in a report of March 1967, says much the same thing, commenting that only a handful of states have moved to meet the problems of their urban areas and that state governments are on the verge of losing control over the mounting problems of central city deterioration and the rapid growth of metropolitan areas.[2] Martin observes further that while the states are critical "of the growing practice of direct dealing between Washington and the cities, which they regard as both a perversion of the federal system and a pointed

---

[1] Roscoe C. Martin, *The Cities and the Federal System* (Atherton Press, 1965), Chap. 6.

[2] Advisory Commission on Intergovernmental Relations, *Eighth Annual Report*, 1967.

threat to state sovereignty," the states have displayed little interest in taking action. "It is not that the states wish to play an active role, but that they wish to be thought of as wishing to."[3]

But the questionableness of the states as instruments of fiscal salvation does not stem alone from their historic disinterest in urban affairs. Wilson and others have been pointing out that it is at the state level that corruption is still most notorious and widespread. "More boodle is flying around with no one watching in state capitals than in city halls; and state governments continue to be badly decentralized, with formal authority divided among a host of semi-autonomous boards, commissions, and departments. The states have rarely been subjected to the kinds of reform which over the years have gradually centralized formal authority in the hands of a professional manager or a single strong mayor."[4]

Economists are, of course, by training more sensitive to violations of economic law than to such nasty transgressions against economic order as corruption—the invisible hand, whatever its other disabili-

---

[3] *Ibid.*, p. 169.

[4] James Q. Wilson, "Corruption: the Shame of the States," *The Public Interest*, Winter 1966, p. 35. See also: William J. Bender, "The Corruption Problem," *National Civic Review*, March 1966; Senator Joseph D. Tydings, "The Last Chance for the States," *Harper's*, March 1966, pp. 71–79; Robert Sherrill, "Florida's Pork Chop Lesiglature," *Harper's*, November 1965, pp. 82–97; "Cleaning Up the Illinois Legislature: a Follow-up Report," by Paul Simon, *Harper's*, September 1965, p. 125; Robert S. Allen (ed.), *Our Sovereign State* (The Vanguard Press, New York, 1949); Trevor Armbristor, "The Octopus in the State House," *Saturday Evening Post*, February 12, 1966; Paul Simon, "A Study in Corruption," *Harper's*, September 1964.

ties, is never caught robbing the till. But surely the propensity toward fiscal propriety, or the lack of it, should be a consideration in selecting a chosen instrument to dispose of the national dividend. To be sure, the degree of corruption is not such as to incapacitate most state governments (the highways do get built) and there are some—a few—which display the inventive and innovational qualities that Heller extols. But one darkly suspects that, on balance, ingenuity and innovation may be used more to get hold of money than to use it for promoting the general welfare.

Finally, there is the question of whether many of the states have the geographic jurisdiction, resources, and general sense of unity and of common interest to deal adequately with the problems of their growing cities and metropolitan areas, let alone the looming problems of megalopolis.[5]

On turning to local governments we find fragmentation, political weakness, and antiquated organization which greatly impair them for useful service as decision-making instruments to meet the problems of this high-flying age. Urban governments, particularly in the older sections of the country, were devised for the conditions of the nineteenth century. Continued population growth, along with the advent of the motor vehicle and other modern communications devices, have made obsolete old urban government boundary lines and have created a complex of problems with which present urban governments were never designed to cope.

---

[5] See Bruce Bahrenburg, "New Jersey's Search for an Identity," *Harper's*, April 1964, pp. 87–90.

The Committee for Economic Development's recent policy statement on Modernizing Local Government says, "American institutions of local government are under severe and increasing strain. . . . Adaptation to change has been so slow, so limited, and so reluctant that the future role—even the continued viability—of these institutions is now in grave doubt."[6] CED's credentials for responsibility and respectability have seldom been questioned, and its deliberations on local government were assisted by the usual pride of academic lions. Therefore we have to pay some attention to indictments such as the following:

Very few local units are large enough—in population, area, or taxable resources—to apply modern methods in solving current and future problems. Even the largest cities find their major problems insoluble because of limits on their geographic areas, their taxable resources, and their legal powers.

Overlapping layers of local governments abound—municipalities, townships, school districts, special districts—which in certain areas may number ten or more. They may all have power to tax the same land, but frequently no one of them has the power to deal with specific urban problems.

Public control of the local governments is ineffective or sporadic, and public interest in local politics is lagging. Contributing factors are the confusion resulting from the many-layered system, profusion of elective offices without policy significance, and increasing mobility of the population.

Most units are characterized by notably weak policy-making and antiquated administrative machinery. Or-

---

[6] CED, *Modernizing Local Government* (1966), p. 8.

ganizational concepts considered axiomatic in American business firms are unrecognized or disregarded in most local governments.

Personnel are notoriously weak. Low prestige of municipal service, low pay scales, and lack of knowledge and appreciation of professional qualifications all handicap the administrative process.[7]

The subject of metropolitan-scale government warrants a further comment. It would appear that some have given up on the possibility of getting effective metropolitan-scale government at all, and it is further asserted that smaller governments have a greater capacity to meet consumer preferences, since it is easier for people to locate in jurisdictions offering service levels which best meet their particular needs (the Tiebout effect). A supporting view is that collective decisions reached by small aggregations of individuals are likely to be more nearly optimal than decisions of larger aggregations. The view is one of the urban governmental process as a two-person game between taxpayers-consumers and governments-suppliers with the taxpayers able to say, "Don't cheat. I know what I dealt you!"

The preference for smaller governments runs into a fact of life: that smaller governments tend to be less efficient and to command less constituent interest than larger governments; local governments in general get less attention from constituents than state governments, and state governments get less than the national government. And it appears that the smaller the government the stronger the veto power of the negative elements therein.

---

[7] *Ibid.*, pp. 11ff.

The plea for "grass roots" government is likely to be in fact a plea for less government. To cite Martin again: " 'Bring government back home' and 'return government to the people' are battle cries equally familiar in the cause of local autonomy and in that of states' rights. . . . In point of fact it is quite clear that the goal sought often is not local autonomy or states' rights as such but rather less government, and moreover government more immediately and more directly subject to control."[8]

If funds are handed out to bodies without competent planning and administrative machinery, there is no particular reason to think that they will be disbursed by any system of considered priorities. They may even be used to reduce taxes, leaving public services unimproved. Nathan, in a recent study for the Committee for Economic Development of probable responses in several low-income states, concludes that this is the most likely outcome in some such states.[9] Well, Heller has said, at least we will have substituted superior and cheaper-to-administer taxes for existing inferior state and local taxes, and this would be a gain. But I submit that it is not much of a gain, considering the fact that the social costs of deficient education and other social services have to be picked up somewhere else, as when the undereducated move into urban centers in wealthier states.

Given such prospects, and such testimonials of

---

[8] *The Cities and the Federal System*, p. 190.

[9] Richard P. Nathan, paper dealing with the potential impact of general aid in four selected states (prepared for the Committee for Economic Development; to be published shortly).

inadequacy, incompetence, and propensity to peculation, are we nonetheless in the position of those who have to patronize the crooked roulette wheel because it is the only one in town?

Surely if federal tax machinery provides the wherewithal for a "national dividend," it would be profligate to use federal funds simply to bolster up existing institutions. If we are going to depend, as I think we must, on the decision-making and innovational capacities of state and local governments, let us seek to improve those capacities. Let us fashion federal grants to achieve this end.

Tying federal grants to minimum standards of administration or planning is nothing new. Thus:

- The Bureau of Public Roads has required federal-aid highways to meet design and construction standards. Pursuant to a 1962 amendment to the federal-aid highway law, the Secretary of Commerce after July 1, 1965, will not approve any program for projects in an urban area of more than 50,000 population unless he finds that such projects are based on a continuing comprehensive planning process carried on co-operatively by state and local communities.
- The Hill-Burton Act of 1946 requires preparation of general state plans for hospital development as a condition of federal grants for hospital construction.
- The Housing Act of 1954 introduced a requirement for comprehensive community planning and the submission of community "workable plans" as a condition of urban renewal grants. While no one would claim that this stipulation has wrought

wonders, while many of the "workable plans" have been rudimentary and the provisions of many have not been complied with, the requirements have undoubtedly made urban governments more aware of the elements of urban renewal and of the virtues of planning, and have touched off a boom in the demand for planners.

A number of recent Congressional acts have undertaken to encourage metropolitan area-wide planning and organization:

· Section 701 of the Housing Law provides planning grants to metropolitan areas. This has led to the establishment of more than one hundred metropolitan planning commissions.
· Legislation providing grants for water pollution control increases the amount of the federal contribution from 30 to 50 per cent of construction costs for a metro-wide plan, as opposed to a purely local-jurisdiction project.
· The Housing Act of 1966 requires that after June 30, 1967, to the extent possible, any local government seeking federal aid for development funds will have to be reviewed by an agency which is designated as a metropolitan or regional planning agency, and further that the designating body to which the planning agency is responsible be composed of elected chief officials of the region. Under the impetus of this legislation several score of these metro-planning agencies have been organized.

Lyle C. Fitch

Agenda for Improved State and Local Government

Most state governments need substantial reor-
ganization and reform of personnel and budgeting
practices if they are effectively to discharge their
decision-making and administrative responsibilities
inherent in the federal system. Most generally
needed items include:

—abolition of quasi-independent administrative
boards and commissions (frequently they have
earmarked funds), insulated from any responsibility for state welfare as a whole;
—concomitantly, centering administrative responsibility in the office of the governor, and equipping
the office with planning, budgeting, and administrative expertise;
—limitation of legislative responsibility to matters
of broad policy and budget approval; abolition
of legislative budgets and exercise of administrative powers by legislatures or by individual legislators;
—comprehensive merit personnel systems;
—comprehensive budgets covering all funds and
expenditure categories, preferably based on program budget concepts (these have been notably
unsuccessful thus far for reasons having little to
do with their intrinsic merits);
—strict conflict-of-interest laws;
—constitutional provisions affording maximum latitude to local governments, which meet reasonable
standards of adequacy.

For an agenda of local government reform, I refer to the CED prescriptions.[10] These include:

—reduction in number of local governments by at least 80 per cent, and severe curtailment of over-lapping layers of local government ("townships and most types of special districts are obvious targets for elimination");
—limitation of popular election to members of legis-lative bodies and the chief executive in the "strong mayor" type of municipal government;
—a single strong executive—elected mayor or city manager;
—modern personnel systems;
—use of county, or combinations of county, juris-dictions to attack metropolitan problems;
—use of federal—and state—grants-in-aid to en-courage local government administrative reforms, particularly reforms having to do with consolida-tion and organization to meet metropolitan prob-lems.

So What Can We Do with Federal Grants?

Having agitated for use of federal grants as in-centives to improve state and local government decision-making and administrative capacities, I must confess to being short of suggestions for ways to accomplish this objective. It would be simple if the federal government could say to the states and localities: "Reorganize; eliminate corruption; intro-duce PPBS (program planning and budgeting sys-

---

[10] In *Modernizing Local Government*, pp. 16ff.

tems); hire good personnel" as a condition for getting per capita grants. But the matter in fact is
not so simple. Consider the job of writing the criteria
of acceptable standards. Then consider the job of
evaluating the states and localities to determine if
they have met the criteria (including allowing for
inevitable time lags). Finally, consider the fights
with state congressional delegations in cases where
it is necessary to determine that a state and its local
governments have not met required standards.

Analogous, if less comprehensive, stipulations have
been made before. True, they have evoked yowls of
protest from offended politicians, as did the requirement for placing unemployment compensation systems under civil service; however, protesters against
improved administration are seldom on the side of
the angels. I therefore think that we can tie federal
grants to needed innovations in governmental organization and administration despite the difficulties
cited above. In the absence of such incentives, the
roadblocks to improvement are, generally speaking,
virtually impassable.

I shall toss out a few suggestions as starting points
for further discussion.

- Let the Congress declare, in a preamble to legislation establishing a national dividend in whatever
  form, that one of the prime objectives of the act
  is to increase the planning, decision-making and
  administrative capacities, as well as the financial
  capacities, of the state and local governments.
- As a condition for receiving grants, the states
  should prepare plans for administrative improve-

ment of state and local government over, say, four-year periods; and thereafter file annual reports of progress in implementing such plans. Plans should address themselves to, among other things, recasting local governments to meet present and emerging problems of urbanism.

· State governments should present plans for using the federal "dividend" payments, such plans to be drawn up in consultation with their major local governments. In California, the League of California Cities has requested the state government to work with the League in preparing plans for the disposition of any federal government unconditional grant. However, I would be skeptical of imposing any rigid requirement of this nature which might end up as an instrument for perpetuating local government structures, forms or practices which need reforming.

· Each state and local government, to qualify for grants, should institute personnel systems based on merit and professional competence. (I have avoided using the term "civil service" in recognition of the fact that many present civil service systems have become rigid, unresponsive, and uncontrollable administrative straitjackets; notwithstanding, the answer still seems to lie in the direction of improving career-service systems rather than abolishing them.)

· The notion of tax "effort" by the states and localities should be built into any formula for federal rebates to the states, providing an inducement for equalization of state and local tax rates relative to ability to pay.

Lyle C. Fitch

The Reuss Bill

A bill (H.R. 1166) introduced in the House of Representatives by Congressman Henry S. Reuss of Wisconsin, on January 10, 1967, seeks the same objectives and for the same reasons set forth in the above discussion. It also is more specific on administrative techniques. Under the Reuss Bill, block grants would be made conditional upon the submission by the states of acceptable programs of government modernization; the review and evaluation bodies would be regional co-ordinating committees and the Advisory Commission on Intergovernmental Relations, which would certify as eligible programs reflecting "sufficient State creative initiative so as to qualify that State for Federal block grants." Among the items to be considered in drawing up such programs are the following:

—arrangements for dealing with interstate regional, including metropolitan, problems;
—strengthening and modernizing state governments;
—strengthening and modernizing local rural, urban, and metropolitan governments;
—proposed uses of federal block grants, including provisions for passing on at least 50 per cent to local governments.

My principal reservation is predicated on a question of whether the ACIR is the most suitable body to make final determinations on acceptable programs. My fear is that this would involve the ACIR in a good many controversies with large amounts of money at stake, and that this might dilute the high quality of the work the ACIR has been doing; it might drastically change the nature of the Advisory Commission on Intergovernmental Relations or even destroy it as an organization. These fears may be exaggerated but such possibilities should be carefully considered, along with alternative administrative arrangements.

Postscript

As we debate the problems of metropolitan areas the urban torrent is overrunning the boundaries of these areas. Jean Gottman some years ago identified a megalopolis stretching from Boston to Norfolk. Wattenberg and Scammon point out that it is "already apparent that the eastern megalopolis will not stand alone for much longer. We can now see the beginnings of other megalopoli in different areas. One is clearly forming along the southwestern end of Lake Michigan. . . . Another, smaller megalopolis is growing from Miami north to Fort Lauderdale and beyond—still another megalopolis may some day connect Los Angeles and San Francisco–Oakland (with Fresno in the middle) . . . and a fifth may eventually link Detroit and Cleveland, with Toledo in the middle, or link Cleveland and Pittsburgh with Youngstown in between."[11]

As Bertram Gross has observed, these complexes will be unprecedented aggregations not only of population but also of wealth, knowledge, and power.

---

[11] Benjamin J. Wattenberg in collaboration with Richard M. Scammon, *This U.S.A.: An Unexpected Family Portrait of 194,067,296 Americans Drawn from the Census* (Doubleday, 1965), p. 87.

Lyle C. Fitch

But this is not to argue for a quantum leap from present forms into megalopolis. It is to remind us that time is running out, and that unless we act to improve planning and decision-making mechanisms the prospect ahead is a continuation and probably an exacerbation of mindless, formless, inefficient, and unbeautiful urban sprawl, inferior government services, and growing frustration with the widening gap between the performance and the potential of the affluent society.

FEDERAL GRANTS TO CITIES, DIRECT AND INDIRECT

Carl S. Shoup [*]

Residents of urban areas want a higher level of government services of the kind that cities and suburban areas provide, and are willing to pay for them. This willingness to pay is, however, only an average; underneath, there lie sharp conflicts between groups of persons at different income and wealth levels within any one urban area. The very poor, for example, want more and better education and more and better housing; those in the same urban area who are on their way up may not be willing to sacrifice much in order to meet these wants of the very poor; and many of those in that same area who have reached the economic heights may be indifferent, not opposing but not promoting.

These conflicts of interest among social and economic groups are often lost sight of in preoccupation with the type of government service that, if made available to anyone in a specified group (usually a geographical group), is supplied to all other members of the group at zero marginal cost per person.[1] Edu-

---

[*] Professor of Economics, Columbia University.

[1] Examples of a government service that can be supplied at zero marginal cost per person are eradication of mosquitoes in a certain area, or a theatre performance. The addition of one more resident to the mosquito-plagued area does not increase the total cost of mosquito eradication, and the departure of one

92

cation, in contrast, is a strictly rationed public service with a positive marginal cost both for level of
service to any given number of persons, and for
number of persons accommodated at any given level
of service. So, too, in large degree, are police protection, fire protection, refuse removal, and hospital
and other medical care (this is not an exhaustive
list). And of course transfer payments, by definition
almost, have a positive marginal money cost.

The average willingness to buy more of these public services is inhibited in expression, to some degree,
by competitive economic relationships among cities
and also among suburban areas, and even between a
city and its suburbs. What all could do easily acting
together, each can do only with difficulty, in a world
of mobile capital and labor, acting separately. The
familiar spillover aspects increase the difficulty with
which the residents of a given urban area can get
what they are willing to pay for, but the importance
of this factor relative to the others mentioned here
may not be quite as great as is often assumed.
Spillins help mitigate the difficulties caused by
spillovers.

All these forces that tend to prevent a given urban

---

person from that area would also not change the total cost.
Accordingly, the marginal cost of supplying the service to persons is zero. Similarly, until the theatre is filled to capacity
(and abstracting from the better views obtained in some parts
of the theatre) the addition or subtraction of one spectator does
not change the cost of the performance.

In all cases of zero marginal cost per person it must be under-
stood that beyond some number of persons there come into play
capacity limits or increased geographical distances that cause an
increase in marginal cost, usually a lumpy increase.

area from getting what it is willing to pay for can be partly overcome by joint action of all urban areas operating through the federal government. To be sure, the non-urban areas are inevitably involved in any such joint action, and it will be assumed in the discussion to follow that their interests are properly taken into account when, for example, a federal tax is increased in order to send grants to state or local units throughout the country.

Joint action by the urban areas through state government channels has proved useful, but it is restricted by the fact that each state contains only a small percentage of the number of urban areas in the country. For purposes of the present discussion, Los Angeles, Chicago, and New York City must work together, or at least work simultaneously, as effectively as must New York City, Buffalo, Rochester, and the other urban areas of New York State. Joint action by residents of the nationwide network of urban areas, through the federal government, is accomplished by paying more federal taxes and getting more federal grants-in-aid than otherwise. The federal government is not only a source of funds but a useful mechanism that the urban areas can employ for joint action.

These statements tend too much to abstract, as suggested above, from the inevitable participation in such a joint-action program of the farm areas and other non-urban areas of the country. But if we look ahead two or three decades, we see an era of farm factories accounting for much of agricultural output, more capital-intensive than most urban activities, and a far larger proportion of the population being in urban (including suburban) areas. While it would be foolish to plan an urban finance program in unreal isolation from non-urban areas, it is a useful intellectual exercise to consider the limiting case, where by hypothesis the country contains only urban-suburban areas and farm-factory areas, and to ask, in those circumstances: Would the present-day problems of urban finance have disappeared? The answer is clearly in the negative.

These necessities and trends foreshadow a decrease in the relative (and I emphasize relative) economic and political importance of the states as suppliers and allocators of funds for the services of education and other rationed public services. In absolute terms, the state governments will continue to grow in economic and political significance, perhaps indeed fairly rapidly. But the urban areas, working jointly through the federal government, will grow relatively more rapidly.

The states can no longer be assumed to be willing or able to pass through all the funds from the federal level that the urban areas want to supply themselves with (using the federal taxing mechanism as an intermediary, producers' good) by their joint action. The chief reason for this unwillingness and inability on the part of any given state is that the joint action must be taken by all the urban areas of the country. It must be more than joint action of all the urban areas within any one state. The beneficial effects of reapportionment emphasized by Walter Heller will not, in this view, be enough.

Accordingly, direct financial contact between the federal government and the several urban areas will have to increase if the urban centers are to act effectively in this joint effort of theirs.

We are therefore at an important crossroads in the fiscal history of the United States. Imaginative, perhaps bold, decisions will be needed if full advantage is to be taken of the possibilities of joint action by urban areas to help themselves. No doubt, state aid, financed in part by federal grants to states, will continue to play a significant role in urban finance. But it is at least questionable whether the states should be used as the only or even the major channel for funds by which urban areas are enabled to help themselves.

The residents of urban areas know pretty well what they want in exchange for the moneys that they will be contributing, through increased federal taxes, to this joint program. Each urban area can usefully be given a high degree of freedom in spending what is, after all, largely its own money, provided only that it is truly acting in the spirit of a joint program. The grants (we should devise a better term for something that will not, for any given urban area, be entirely, or even chiefly, a gift from others) should be made conditional, not so much on what the urban areas do with the money, as on what they do with themselves.

Acting in the spirit of a joint program means, *inter alia*, that each urban area plans and acts jointly within its own economic and political boundaries, to the best of its ability. Annexation of suburbs to a core city is not needed, at least not universally; many other forms of joint action within a given urban area are available. A cluster of several core cities together with their respective suburbs do not need to become one huge politically monolithic metropolis. But if a given core city and its suburbs, or a cluster of such core cities and their suburbs, is to expect all other similar aggregates in the United States to work with it through the federal machinery of increased federal taxation and increased federal grants, it must not itself act as a jostling group of fragmented economic units.

Even with unrestricted use, the grants would retain some element of specification. A nominally block grant to a subordinate political unit is implicitly a somewhat specified grant, since a subordinate political unit, by definition, cannot operate over as wide a range at its own discretion as can the unit to which it is subordinate. The extreme illustration of this point is seen in Ruggles' interesting suggestion that federal grants be made to local school boards. These could be termed block grants, that is, general-purpose grants, to be used as the school boards thought fit—within their range of power.

The general-purpose but co-operation–conditioned grants routed through the federal government will be most effective in overcoming the three problems mentioned above—conflicts of interest, restraints imposed by economic competition, and spillovers—if they are distributed by formulae that take account of three factors:

—Need (for example, the percentage of population consisting of children of school age);
—Ability (for example, yield per head of a standard-type standard-rate tax system);

97

—Effort (for example, some modified version of the formula, local tax revenues per capita divided by local income per capita).

General-purpose, co-operation–conditioned grants need not and, to get the most out of a dollar transferred, should not be simple per capita distributions.

But if ability and effort are to be measurable realistically, the urban areas must be given, by their states, more freedom to impose what taxes they want to impose, and must be induced to take more responsibility for their own fiscal health. This does not mean creating the equivalent of more states; it may well mean a quite novel form of fiscal relationship of urban area to state.

In 1951, when Robert Murray Haig and I were analyzing New York City's financial problem, I suggested that the continual irritation, responsibility-dodging, and unseemly charges of short-changing and greed that at that time marked the relations of New York City with Albany might at some time in the future be eliminated, to the benefit of all parties, by a compact whereby New York State would abstain from taxing New York City residents and business firms and would give New York City the power to levy any taxes that the state could levy, in return for which New York City would give up all grants from the state and would itself pay an annual block grant to the state.[2]

This formula was analyzed in considerable detail by Jackson Phillips, who concluded, quite rightly I believe, that there should be no attempt to make

---

[2] "A New Fiscal System for New York City," unpublished memorandum, March 22, 1951.

New York City a (then) 49th state, "because of the history and tradition which bind City and State."[3] The state would give exclusive taxing power to the city over city residents and taxable events occurring in the city, but would, in Phillips' formulation of the plan, retain a veto power over future uses of new tax bases by the city. The city would surrender all rights to existing or future state grants but would be free to accept federal grants. The city would pay to the state an annual block grant computed on the basis of (a) the city's fair share of the state's cost of equalization (this fair share was, at least in the 1950's, deemed to be a positive amount), plus (b) the cost of services performed by the state for the city's benefit, minus (c) the city's cost of providing services for New York State residents living in Nassau, Rockland, Westchester, and Suffolk counties and for New Jersey residents of the metropolitan area.

I commend Phillips' thoughtful analysis to your attention, not on an assumption that this particular blueprint is still the best way to give New York City the fiscal power and responsibility that it needs, for I have not restudied this issue in detail since then—though it still appeals to me as being a possible solution at some time over the next few decades—but because it illustrates the kind of novel approach, a partial breaking with tradition both here and elsewhere, that may be needed if urban finances in the United States are to be as vastly improved as they can be.

---

[3] Jackson R. D. Phillips, "Intergovernmental Fiscal Relations and the City of New York," doctoral dissertation, Columbia University, 1957, p. 274.

COMMENTS ON BLOCK GRANTS TO THE STATES

*Harvey E. Brazer**

Among the expressions of opposition to the "Heller Plan," two related objections appear to me to have gained most support. These are the contention that the states cannot be relied upon to spend block grants in accord with national priorities, and that the states cannot be trusted to take proper cognizance of the needs of local governments in the allocation of block grant funds.

Typical of the first of these objections is Richard Musgrave's view that: "There should be some assurance that funds, which originate at the national level, will be spent according to national priorities. Lacking this relationship, the revenue transfer may well result in a Balkanization of our expenditure structure, at the very time when a comprehensive national approach to public service programs is most needed."[1] He prefers, apparently, to leave the states and their local subdivisions to their own resources except insofar as the tastes or preferences of the people living in those jurisdictions, as reflected in the policies of their legislative representatives, may coincide with the

---

* Professor of Economics, The University of Michigan.
[1] R. A. Musgrave, "National Taxes and Local Needs," *The Nation*, January 16, 1967, p. 80.

preferences of the nation as a whole as expressed in the policies that the national Administration and the Congress choose to pursue.

This line of argument seems to imply that the states are unlikely to spend funds received from the federal government in the form of block grants or unconditional subsidies in a manner that adequately reflects social priorities. Not knowing what those priorities are and being reluctant to base a judgment on the matter on my own preference orderings, I can neither confirm nor deny that implication. But it may be instructive to look at the disposition that the states did make of the increase in general revenues they realized in the decade between 1955 and 1965.

The relevant data are presented in Table 1. General revenue from all sources increased from $16.2 billion in 1955 to $40.9 billion in 1965. One-third of this increase of $24.7 billion went into state aid to local jurisdictions and a further 28 per cent was absorbed by increased direct state expenditures for health and hospitals, welfare, and education, to account for almost two-thirds of the gain in revenue. With respect to highways, we may assume that state expenditures are financed out of earmarked taxes and federal grants-in-aid. Deducting the increases of $4.3 billion and $0.7 billion in state direct expenditures and state aid for highways, respectively, from the increase in general revenue, leaves $19.7 billion. Of this sum ($19.7 billion), which appears to me to be more relevant than the total increase of $24.7 billion, the increase in state aid for purposes other than highways represented 38 per cent and the increase in direct expenditures for health and hospitals,

TABLE 1
State Revenues and Expenditures, 1955 and 1965

Revenues and Expenditures	1955 ($ billion)	1955 (per cent)	1965 ($ billion)	1965 (per cent)	Increase ($ billion)	Increase (per cent)	Rate of growth (per cent)
GENERAL REVENUES							
Total	16.2	100.0	40.9	100.0	24.7	100.0	9.7
From own sources	13.2	81.5	30.6	74.8	17.4	70.4	8.8
Federal aid	2.8	17.1	9.9	24.1	7.1	28.8	13.6
STATE AID	6.0	37.0	14.2	34.6	8.2	33.1	9.0
DIRECT GENERAL EXPENDITURES							
Total	11.2	100.0	26.1	100.0	15.0	100.0	8.9
Health and hospitals	1.3	12.0	2.7	10.3	1.4	9.1	7.3
Welfare	1.6	14.3	3.0	11.5	1.4	9.4	6.5
Education	1.9	17.0	6.2	23.6	4.3	28.6	12.5
Highways	3.9	34.8	8.2	31.4	4.3	28.9	7.7
Other	2.4	21.9	6.0	23.1	3.6	24.1	9.5

Sources: U.S. Bureau of the Census, *Census of Governments, 1962*, Vol. VI, No. 4, *Historical Statistics on Governmental Finances and Employment*, p. 41; *idem, Governmental Finances in 1964–65*, pp. 20–23.

welfare, and education 36 per cent. Thus in total almost three-quarters of the sum available for non-highway purposes was allocated to the three named functions and local jurisdictions.

Clearly, the disposition of funds in the past offers no certain assurance as to their disposition in the future, but it is at least suggestive. Moreover, the data presented here do not provide an unequivocal picture of the use by the states of revenues over which legislatures had full discretionary control. Virtually all of the $7.1 billion increase in federal aid, of which almost half was for highways, was in the form of conditional grants-in-aid, and a substantial proportion of state non-highway taxes are earmarked, either for distribution to local governments or for specific direct state use. In the absence of an elaborate refinement of the data that would permit more definitive conclusions, it is possible only to hazard the guess that the largest part of the increase in unencumbered state receipts went to education, health and hospitals (primarily mental health), and correctional institutions.

Thus if we can accept recent trends as offering some, albeit insufficient, evidence as to how new unrestricted state receipts might be used, I see little justification for the fear that the states cannot be relied upon to make "appropriate" use of federal block grants.

The second objection stems from the view that the most urgent needs in the public sector are to be found in our urban communities and that the states cannot be trusted to take proper cognizance of these needs. Thus, many of those who support the general principles of the Heller Plan would insist that the funds be used solely to support education or that the states be required to distribute a minimum proportion of the amounts received to local jurisdictions.[2]

It seems to me, however, that distribution to cities, or a uniform proportion required to be distributed to local governments, involves serious and perhaps insuperable difficulties. The states vary widely in the distribution of functional responsibilities between the state and its local subdivisions. In 1965, in the United States as a whole, the states accounted for 35 per cent of total state-local direct general expenditure for all functions, but this proportion ranged from 22 and 24 per cent in New York and New Jersey to between 60 and 75 per cent in West Virginia, Vermont, Alaska, and Hawaii.[3] Thus, a requirement that, say, 50 per cent of a federal block grant be distributed to local jurisdictions within each state would be overly generous for those jurisdictions in the latter group of states, whereas it would fall far below the proportion of expenditure obligations now carried by local jurisdictions in New York and New Jersey, as well as many other states. Obviously, any other uniform proportion would suffer from the same kind of disability. It is only within each of the states taken as a whole that all state-local functions are more or less uniformly as-

---

[2] One or other of these requirements was a feature of several bills providing for block grants or revenue sharing introduced in the 1966 session of Congress. See, for example, H.R. 4070 (Representative Charles E. Goodell of New York), and S. 3405 (Senator Jack Miller of Iowa).

[3] U.S. Bureau of the Census, *Governmental Finances in 1964–65*, pp. 34–38.

sumed. It follows, therefore, that block grants or unconditional subsidies should be distributed to the states for further distribution, as they may choose, to their local subdivisions.

It is undeniable that state legislatures have, in the past, been dominated by rural interests, leading to the neglect of urban problems and urban needs. But the reapportionment decision of the Supreme Court in 1962 has already corrected this condition in two-thirds of the states and the process can be expected to have been completed very soon. With reapportionment, the voices of the cities and their suburbs should be adequately heard by the time the Congress has moved favorably on block grants to the states.

One need only look at the contrasts to be found among cities in the responsibilities they assume to recognize that federal block grants to these jurisdictions would be impossible to devise in a manner that would do reasonable justice to even a substantial portion of them. New York City, for example, is a very different creature from Chicago. In 1965 New York City spent $432 per capita, the City of Chicago, $113.[4] New York finances all or part of some of the most costly functions of government which in Chicago are financed through the state, the county, the school district, and several special districts. Thus any given amount in a block grant that would be meaningful in magnitude to New York would be an excessively generous bonanza to Chicago. Needless to say, most cities in the United States would fall somewhere in between these two extremes. The vast

---

[4] U.S. Bureau of the Census, *City Government Finances, 1964–65*, pp. 21, 38.

diversity in their circumstances and in responsibilities assumed by cities within states, let alone among the several states, is so great as to defy any attempt by the Congress to design a uniform, reasonable system of block grants.

None of the foregoing is meant to deny the existence of major unmet needs at the local level of government, particularly in our urban communities. And, in my judgment, the states and, *through the states*, the federal government should contribute far more than they now do to meeting the costs of public services supplied by cities and other local jurisdictions. It seems equally clear to me, however, that direct federal grants to local governments should remain limited in scope and designed, in the form of grants-in-aid, to cope with specific deficiencies relating to functional areas that are of overwhelming concern to the nation as a whole.

REBUTTAL COMMENTS

Walter W. Heller

Anyone who advances a proposal that gets labeled with his own name is assumed to have a vested— and perhaps even irrational—interest in that proposal. I plead guilty, but perhaps not to the misdemeanor you may have in mind. For my vested interest is not in the specific ins and outs of a particular plan, but in two broad objectives:

—first, to focus national interest and concern on the revitalization of our state-local governments as an essential step toward a stronger federalism;
—second, and closely interrelated, to find ways and means of sharing federal revenue bounties with state and local governments that will loosen their fiscal fetters and help them exercise and strengthen their muscles—and do so in ways that will increase the progressivity of our public revenue-expenditure system.

The first aim is already well on the way to accomplishment. There's a pretty brisk national dialogue under way, and the conference which produced these papers is part of it.

To accomplish the second aim, I like income tax sharing for reasons that to my mind are persuasive and have yet to be effectively refuted. But let me make crystal clear that I regard a number of variants as quite acceptable, and that federal income tax credits—which I have advocated since 1941—could be a mighty good second best.

I am concerned, however, that those who share my general aims may lose sight of them in their zeal to achieve certain *specific* objectives through the use of federal moneys, or in their fear that some of the funds freely shared with states would be put to poor uses, or, in some cases, in their desire to display their talents as critics. Those who insist on near-perfection as a necessary condition for action are the enemies of progress, here as elsewhere.

In my paper, I have listed the six criteria or tests that a plan for channeling new sources of funds to the states must meet. Unless and until someone comes forward with persuasive arguments that these criteria are not valid, or that other and supervening criteria should be applied, or that revenue sharing or something akin to it is inferior to other instruments to carry out the six stated purposes, I see no reason to forsake tax sharing or general assistance without hamstrings attached.

Yet, the growing dialogue has suggested some significant modifications or conditions within the general no-strings framework. The conference discussion has underscored the importance of assuring a fair slice of the proceeds to the urban places, an area left unresolved in the tax-sharing plan at earlier stages. My paper reflects an acceptance of this modification.

Lyle Fitch casts doubt on the whole no-strings approach on the basis of the inefficiency and often unsavory behavior of state and local governments. His observations as a long-time, perceptive participant in state-local affairs must be respected. But they are bound to be impressionistic—as are mine. All told, as I spell out in *New Dimensions*, the inefficiency argument is overdone. And as to misuse of funds, this fear seems more an argument against *any* federal subvention at all than one against tax sharing as such.

It is easy to criticize the scale and quality of state and local government. But it is very hard to refute the basic proposition that they are financially under-nourished and that general support of their efforts would mean expansion of the public sector. Furthermore, it is highly likely that this expansion of the public sector would come at the expense of income tax cuts and not at the expense of federal programs.

Next, I would stress that revenue sharing or some derivative or modification of it is not to be judged as an all-or-nothing proposition standing by itself. I view it as part of a three-ply solution for a three-ply problem: (1) federal operations for public activities that obviously have to be conducted at the federal level; (2) categorical grants-in-aid for operations at the state-local level involving significant spillover effects and hence a national interest; (3) some form of revenue sharing particularly to support the more exclusively state-local allocative functions, in Musgrave's terms, and to strengthen the fabric of state-local government.

And I am also compelled to point out that federal programs operating under Ruggles' suggested approach are something less than an unblemished success. Tied aid, all too often, is the tie that binds rather than liberates. Granted, categorical aids are vital, and sharing must be a supplement, not a substitute for them. This again suggests that a combination of ingredients—including a revenue-sharing program that would sluice, not down the drain but into productive state-local uses, some $6 billion a year—provides the best remedy for the ailment of the fiscal mismatch.

As to Lyle Fitch's concluding comments, it seems to me that while one can argue that some other network of regional and local governments might be more efficient, my guess is we have to live with the one we've got. Given our long-held political values—values of decentralization, political diversity, and experimentation—it seems to me you have to find some way to serve them more effectively within the existing framework of federalism. What better way than for the federal government to return part of its (prospectively) unneeded revenues, not to the private sector to use as it pleases in pursuit of second-order private wants but to the state-local sector to use as it pleases in pursuit of first-order public needs?

Richard Ruggles

It has been suggested that since revenue sharing is just one of three approaches, and since it is only a small amount, it is a useful adjunct to other forms of government finance. Such an argument is not valid since, in fact, revenue sharing is an alternative to doing other things in an area where we need resources, that is, the public sector.

In particular, the argument about the limited nature and concept of revenue sharing works the other way, too. If revenue sharing is to be only a small amount—the four or five billion dollars originally suggested by Walter Heller—it may not be very important to the states.

However, the basic principles are extremely important. Many federal aid programs relate to opportunities that are provided by government to individuals. This brings us head-on to the question of how much of the expenditures of state and local governments are concerned with what I would call national values; we wish to educate the Negro, not just because of the spillover effect, but because we consider such education to be a national value.

Now, in this total governmental mix I would suggest that state and local governments should be in the position of *supplementing* national values from their own resources. In effect, local taxes should provide what the people in the area want over and above the minimum supported by national resources for national programs. This means that if the citizens of a given area want a higher educational level than is provided for by national funds, they can pay for the additional amount over and above the national minimum out of their own resources. On the other hand, local services of a non-national character—police, fire, street cleaning, and so on—should be paid by local communities completely out of local resources. Property taxes are a proper source of revenue for many purposes. We should not lose sight of this.

The federal government has neglected many national values and is only now coming to the point where it is worried about such problems as health and education. If the role of the federal government in these areas is enlarged, then perhaps the states and localities can spend their resources on other needs as they see fit.

The level of government that can best handle any given problem should be relied upon to do so. Otherwise, I think the automatic sluicing of federal funds to states, far from contributing to the national purpose, may in fact be funds down the drain.

Our national program should not be a mere political combination of ingredients, relying on a little bit of this and a little bit of that. To suggest that adopting a state-local pass-through under a revenue-sharing plan would make the plan more palatable is, I think, begging the answer. The fungibility of funds is such that regulations from above are very difficult to enforce, especially if the federal program of revenue sharing is small in relation to both the total of federal aid programs and state and local programs.

So, in conclusion, I would reiterate that I, like Walter Heller, am concerned with the problems of the public sector and how best we can accomplish national objectives in the areas of health, education, and welfare; but that I believe if the federal government does its part in sharing not only the costs but also specific burdens in these areas, this will create enough relief for state and local communities to enable them to devote their resources to more local concerns.

Designed by Gerard A. Valerio

*Composed in Caslon O.S. by
Monotype Composition Company*

*Printed offset by Murray Printing Company
on 60 lb. Allied Offset*

*Cloth bound by Moore and Company
Paper bound by Murray Printing Company*